EAT W

Marika Hanbury
1938 and has bee
perimenting with recipes for as long as she can remember. She never had a domestic science training but learnt the hard way, by trial and error, and is still learning.

Married to explorer and farmer, Robin Hanbury Tenison, she now travels with him to little-known areas of the world. They have two children and live in a fourteenth-century farmhouse high up on Bodmin Moor. Apart from *Eat Well and Be Slim* she has written *Deep-freeze Cookery* (also published by Pan Books), *Soups and Hors d'oeuvres* and *Leftover for Tomorrow*, as well as numerous articles for several magazines, including *Nova*, *Woman* and the *Observer* Colour Magazine. She is now Cookery Editor for the *Sunday Telegraph* and frequently appears on Westward Television.

Also available in Pan Books

ALL ABOUT COOKERY – Mrs Beeton
NEW CASSEROLE TREASURY – Lousene Rousseau Brunner
THE CORDON BLEU BOOK OF JAMS, PRESERVES AND PICKLES – Rosemary Hume and Muriel Downes
THE GEORGE BERNARD SHAW VEGETARIAN COOK BOOK – Mrs Alice Laden, *ed* R. J. Minney
QUICK AND EASY CHINESE COOKING – Kenneth Lo
HERBS FOR HEALTH AND COOKERY – Clare Loewenfeld and Philippa Back
SPANISH COOKING AT HOME AND ON HOLIDAY – Maite Manjón and Catherine O'Brien
THE POULTRY AND GAME COOK BOOK – Ruth Martin
LEARNING TO COOK – Marguerite Patten
WORLD COOKERY – Marguerite Patten
THE MARGARET POWELL COOKERY BOOK
MISS READ'S COUNTRY COOKING
THE CONSTANCE SPRY COOKERY BOOK – Constance Spry and Rosemary Hume
DEEP-FREEZE COOKERY – Marika Hanbury Tenison

EAT WELL AND BE SLIM

MARIKA HANBURY TENISON

A PAN ORIGINAL

PAN BOOKS LTD : LONDON

In association with the
SUNDAY TELEGRAPH

First published 1974 by Pan Books Ltd,
33 Tothill Street, London SW1

ISBN 0 330 23900 7

Made and printed in Great Britain by
Cox & Wyman Ltd, London, Reading and Fakenham

Contents

The Principles of the Book

Like most women, I am easily flattered – one of the things which flatters me most and gives me a glow of satisfaction is when somebody says 'How do you stay so slim?', with the implication that the fact is surprising and, quite rightly, imagining that (*a*) I find it hard to keep thin, and (*b*) I manage to keep my weight down despite temptation.

I do have a tendency to put on weight and to be honest I frequently top what I consider to be my perfect weight by at least half a stone, three or four times a year. Putting it on is no problem – taking it off is something else again and a hard battle.

I have all the problems. I'm a compulsive eater who longs for hunks of bread and dripping when anything goes wrong; I love food and am congenitally greedy; I have a capacity for eating which rivals that of a starved hippopotamus and I could happily live on pâté de foie gras, three courses of pasta and cream cakes for the rest of my life. Perhaps fortunately for me, I also get almost suicidal at the gain of so much as a pound – the only factor which prevents me from blossoming into the 'largest lady in the world'. So I do, you see, know the problems and I learnt them in a hard school.

Being a cookery writer obviously imposes a strain on the system. One is constantly tasting new dishes, searching for new ideas, eating one's own and other people's food with a view to the next article; each day is a ceaseless nibble.

Despite my trade, I somehow manage to win the battle and this is in fact what *Eat Well and Be Slim* is all about. This book is a collection of the recipes I use most frequently in my own home, recipes geared to good food which appeals to the palate, is attractive and satisfying but which will not put on weight. It is not a 'slimming' book because it contains no faddy or crash diets and it does not lay down a rigid pattern of calorie consumption per day and per meal; but it does consist of recipes which keep the weight controlled and are a deterrent to increasing it. It is a family book because it contains recipes which I feel will appeal to both children and adults. Few people are amongst that category that just don't put on weight whatever they eat and I am convinced it is just as important for my husband and children to keep slim as it is for me – they feel better and look better.

If you happen to have been on a strictly limited diet and then use this book, you may find you gain a pound or two; if, on the other hand, you have been eating the average diet of most households, with a fairly high proportion of fats, starches and sugar, the chances are that within a week of using this book you will find an agreeable weight loss.

There is absolutely no need at all for delicious food to be a problem for those with a weight conscience; good food doesn't need to be smothered in rich, creamy sauces or dripping in butter; good food doesn't need to be deep fried in lard or oil; potatoes are not a necessary adjunct to every meal (or indeed any meal) and bread, flour or rice are not essential ingredients to everyday diets.

The recipes in this book were collected with a view to family cooking and to entertaining; there is nothing kinky or way out about them. You may notice that sour cream and yoghurt (much lower in calories and cholesterol than raw cream) are used to replace cream in sauces and soups; that egg yolks are used as a thickening ingredient in the place of flour whenever possible, and that olive oil is used instead of fat or butter whenever possible, but apart from these ingredients the book has no tricks. Its strength lies in the fact that if you want to keep your own and your family's weight down, here is a cookery book which offers you no temptations; which covers every course and type of meal and which provides you with a very wide range of non-fattening dishes. There is no magic in this book apart from the natural magic which enables one to eat well, stay slim and feed a hundred times better than you would on a diet which leaves you a pound or two heavier in weight and heart at the end of the day.

Over the years I have tried everything from eating grapefruits by the ton to living off bananas and milk. In the end it always comes back to the same thing – to avoid putting on weight one must avoid eating fattening foods, have two green vegetables in the place of a portion of potatoes; cut out sweet puddings, avoid rich sauces and deep-fried foods and stick to balanced meals.

I am no professional dietician and I have not studied medicine, but over my years as a cookery writer I have studied the balance of foods which we need to keep us lively and healthy without being overweight. On the whole this balance can be obtained without large intakes of those foods which are fattening.

The most fattening foods, carbohydrates (i.e. starches and sugars) and fats, are usually required by the body to give instant energy but their intake and the amounts required by an individual are governed by the life led by that individual. A dock worker, for instance, using up a great amount of energy a day in physical labour, will require a vast quantity of carbohydrates compared to the office worker; a growing child who is of an athletic mentality will need a higher intake than a middle-aged housewife who has only her home to look after.

On the whole, though, with the coming of the motor car, the practice of longer holidays, more relaxation and more sedentary lives, most of us eat more than we should and a good many of us could well afford to lose the odd pound or two. Therefore, I have concentrated, in this collection of recipes, on those which do not add to the physical load and which do not provide temptation – if recipes for starchy, quick energy-giving foods, are required, they can easily be found in a hundred or more other cookery books. I feel that the olive oil, fats and carbohydrates used in these recipes for cooking, thickening and flavouring, are quite adequate for the average requirement.

Other foods which are required to keep the body healthy and in good condition are as follows:

Protein which can be found in the lean part of meat, fish, dairy products and eggs.

Calcium which can be found in milk products, meat, green vegetables, tomatoes and most fruit, fish and shellfish.

Iron which can be found in liver and kidneys, poultry and game, meat, green vegetables, most fruits, eggs and fish.

Vitamin C which can be found in citrus fruit, blackcurrants, green vegetables, watercress, parsley and milk products.

Vitamin A which can be found in butter, milk and milk products, liver, green vegetables, carrots, tomatoes, eggs, most fruit and oily fish.

Vitamin B which can be found in milk products, eggs, meat, bacon and ham, fish and shellfish, green vegetables, tomatoes and most fruit.

Vitamin D which can be found in animal fats, milk, eggs, herrings, mackerel, salmon and kippers.

On the whole, your health, weight and the condition of your hair, nails and skin are the best pointers to whether or not you are enjoying a sensible and satisfactory diet; if these are not in perfect condition for your age, something is lacking in your diet and it is wise to see a doctor at once.

A Few Pointers

MAKING FOOD ATTRACTIVE

All food seems to taste better and is more enjoyable if it is attractively served and if a little trouble has been taken to make the dish look nice. A little care with last minute garnishing and the arrangement of ingredients can make all the difference to the taste of the whole meal.

GARNISHING

Fresh, bright green parsley, finely chopped and scattered over a dish at the last minute before serving gives it a fresh look.

Colourless dishes can be made to sparkle by the garnish of a colourful ingredient such as finely chopped red peppers, thinly sliced tomatoes or a topping of cheese browned quickly under a grill until it is bubbling and golden.

Cold food can be made more appealing by a surround of chopped aspic, sprigs of watercress glistening with a light coating of vinaigrette dressing or thin slices of cool cucumber.

CHOPPING AND SLICING

Chopping correctly is one of the secrets of good cooking. 'Finely chopped' docs mean *fine* and not hacked into rough pieces. Use a sharp knife and cut the ingredients into very small, uniform pieces. Chop parsley by putting the heads into a mug and snipping with scissors until they are almost powder.

When a recipe calls for dice or cubes, make sure these are all of the same size. When slicing use a very sharp knife or a slicing machine and again make sure all the slices are the same thickness.

SERVING

Hot food must be served hot, on hot plates, or much of the flavour will be lost. It is much better to re-heat a dish if necessary than to keep it simmering away in an oven for hours longer than it should.

Cold food, in the same way, must be served well chilled and here I even go so far as to chill my plates as well. Keep cold food in the refrigerator until the very last minute before it is required; return it to the refrigerator when everyone has been served so that second helpings too will be at the right temperature.

USING THE RIGHT INGREDIENTS

Nothing beats fresh ingredients. Use fresh rather than dried herbs whenever possible; fresh vegetables in season and fresh lemon juice at all times.

Avoid over-seasoning food as this makes one thirsty and sharpens the appetite.

USEFUL KITCHEN GADGETS

A good deal of the time, I find modern kitchen gadgets highly overrated but there are a few well worth investing in: an electric liquidizer, a hand electric whisk, a mouli food mill for puréeing and sieving and a hand-operated manual or electric food slicer.

MISCELLANEOUS

Lemons warmed in an oven for a few minutes will yield more juice.

1 envelope (1 tablespoon, heaped, or $\frac{1}{2}$ oz) gelatine is enough to set 1 pint of liquid. In very hot weather a little extra gelatine may be used.

Washing peeled onions under cold running water helps to prevent crying when chopping them.

If tomatoes or peaches are to be peeled, place them in boiling water for a minute and the skins will slide off with ease.

When making stock from water and stock cubes, add a tablespoon of tomato purée to give a rich flavour.

ALL THE INGREDIENTS IN THESE RECIPES ARE FOR FOUR SERVINGS UNLESS OTHERWISE STATED.

Some Ingredients Used Throughout the Book

If a recipe does not work out quite to your liking, don't be too hasty in blaming the writer – it may be the ingredients you are using. Like all cooks, I have my fads and here are a few notes on the special ingredients I use in many of the recipes.

Mustard: In many dishes, mustard adds a definite flavour or helps to blend with other ingredients to give a faint, almost indefinable taste. Mostly, I use French Dijon mustard, a fairly mild and very yellow variety.

Vinegar: Malt vinegar, of fish and chip fame, has a harsh and rather strong taste. In all my recipes, I use a French brand of white wine vinegar which is clear, light and which blends well with other ingredients.

Pepper: I consider that pepper is one of the most important of seasonings and in almost all recipes I have specifically stated 'freshly ground black pepper' as this has far more flavour and body to it than fine ground white pepper. Freshly grinding the pepper releases the flavours from the corns which is so often lost in pepper which has been pre-ground and left to stand for some time.

Herbs: Whenever possible, I like to use fresh herbs, which have a totally different flavour from the dried varieties. Herbs can be grown in such a small space that even if you do not boast a garden, a small window box or even some plants in pots on the kitchen window-sill can completely revolutionize your cooking. If dried herbs do have to be used, soak them in a little warm water or lemon juice for 5–10 minutes before adding them to the recipe – this will help to release the natural flavouring and scents.

CONVERSION TABLES

International Measures

Measure	*UK*	*Australia*	*New Zealand*	*Canada*
1 pint	20 fl oz	20 fl oz	20 fl oz	20 fl oz
1 cup	10 fl oz	8 fl oz	8 fl oz	8 fl oz
1 tablespoon	$\frac{5}{8}$ fl oz	$\frac{1}{2}$ fl oz	$\frac{1}{2}$ fl oz	$\frac{1}{2}$ fl oz
1 dessertspoon	$\frac{2}{5}$ fl oz	no official measure	—	—
1 teaspoon	$\frac{1}{5}$ fl oz	$\frac{1}{8}$ fl oz	$\frac{1}{6}$ fl oz	$\frac{1}{6}$ fl oz

Conversion of fluid ounces to metric

1 fl oz	=	2.84 millilitres
35 fl oz (approx $1\frac{3}{4}$ Imperial pints)	=	1 litre (1000 ml or 10 decilitres)
1 Imperial pint (20 fl oz)	=	approx 600 ml (6 dl)
$\frac{1}{2}$ Imperial pint (10 fl oz)	=	300 ml (3 dl)
$\frac{1}{4}$ Imperial pint (5 fl oz)	=	150 ml ($1\frac{1}{2}$ dl)
4 tablespoons ($2\frac{1}{2}$ fl oz)	=	70 ml (7 centilitres)
2 tablespoons ($1\frac{1}{4}$ fl oz)	=	35 ml ($3\frac{1}{2}$ cl)
1 tablespoon ($\frac{5}{8}$ fl oz)	=	18 ml (2 cl)
1 dessertspoon ($\frac{2}{5}$ fl oz)	=	12 ml
1 teaspoon ($\frac{1}{5}$ fl oz)	=	6 ml

(All the above metric equivalents are approximate)

Conversion of solid weights to metric

2 lb 3 oz	=	1 k (kilogram)
1 lb	=	453 gm (grammes)
15 oz	=	425 gm
10 oz	=	283 gm
5 oz	=	141 gm
4 oz	=	113 gm
3 oz	=	85 gm
2 oz	=	56 gm
1 oz	=	28 gm

Equivalents

1 UK (old BSI standard) cup equals 1¼ cups in Commonwealth countries
4 UK tablespoons equal 5 Commonwealth tablespoons
5 UK teaspoons equal 6 New Zealand or 6 Canada or 8 Australian
1 UK dessertspoon equals ⅔ UK tablespoon or 2 UK teaspoons

Oven temperatures

Description	*Electric Setting*	*Gas Mark*
Cool	225°F (110°C)	¼
	250°F (130°C)	½
Slow	275°F (140°C)	1
	300°F (150°C)	2
Very moderate	325°F (170°C)	3
	350°F (180°C)	4
Moderate	375°F (190°C)	5
Moderately hot	400°F (200°C)	6
Hot	425°F (220°C)	7
	450°F (230°C)	8
Very hot	475°F (240°C)	9

These temperatures are only an approximate guide as all ovens vary slightly, according to the make and country of manufacture.

Nibbles between meals

Sometimes, the urge to eat between meals is irresistible; the important thing, if you have to have a nibble, is to take a bite of something which will satisfy your hunger pangs but not put on those ounces and pounds which are such agony to take off. Go for snacks which are non-fattening, take time to prepare and look attractive without being full of calories.

Choose from the following ideas:

CELERY STICKS WITH CREAM CHEESE AND GHERKINS

Combine some cream or cottage cheese with finely chopped gherkins and a light seasoning of salt and freshly ground black pepper or cayenne. Fill short lengths of tender celery stalks with the mixture and eat them slowly.

CARROT STICKS WITH CREAM CHEESE DIP

Peel some carrots and cut them into thin matchstick lengths. Crisp the carrots in iced water for 15 minutes. Combine some cream cheese with a tablespoon tomato ketchup, a few drops of Worcestershire sauce and a dash of Tabasco, mix well, pile the sauce into a dish and surround with the carrot sticks.

GREEN PEPPER WITH GARLIC YOGHURT

Remove the core and seeds from a green pepper and cut the flesh into thin strips. Crisp the green pepper in iced water for 15 minutes. Add 2 cloves of garlic, squeezed through a garlic press, to the yoghurt, season with salt and pepper and chill well. Dip the green pepper sticks into the garlic yoghurt.

APPLE AND CHEESE SANDWICHES

Peel firm, crisp eating apples and cut them into thin slices. Dip the apple slices into lemon juice to prevent browning. Sandwich the slices of apple with thin slices of Cheddar cheese in the centre.

CUCUMBER STUFFED WITH COTTAGE CHEESE AND OLIVES

Peel a cucumber and cut into half lengthways. Cut into sections about 2 inches long and scoop out the seeds. Sprinkle with salt and leave to stand for 20 minutes. Drain off excess liquid and fill the hollowed cucumber with a mixture of cottage cheese, chopped black olives and finely chopped spring onions or chives lightly seasoned with salt and pepper.

Simple and sophisticated soups to get a meal off to a good start

HOT SOUPS

Whatever the time of the year, hot soups are always a success, both with the young and the old. They need a light touch and a real feeling for food but in principle are usually surprisingly easy to produce. For sheer value for money, I find vegetable soups about the most satisfactory dishes a housewife can produce; they warm, they nourish and, unless they are packed out with cream or made with a butter and flour base, they are not fattening food.

Often the flavouring of a soup is incorporated in the ingredients which are used in it, but the essential goodness and ultimate success of the dish often depends on the stock used to make it and a home-made stock, rich in vegetable and meaty goodness, beats anything which comes out of a cube or a packet.

Hot soup must be served really hot, in bowls or soup plates which have been pre-heated. Garnishing should be added at the very last minute.

COLD SOUPS

Few things are more pleasant as a starter for a summer lunch or dinner than a well-chilled and delicately flavoured soup, served in attractive soup bowls or cups. Chill the soup for at least two hours in a refrigerator before serving and, if the weather is really hot, add a cube or two of ice to each bowl just before serving.

The colour of cold soups is most important. They must be clear, skimmed of all fat if necessary and the garnishing should be fresh and attractive.

GARNISHES FOR HOT SOUPS

Avoid garnishes that incorporate bread or starchy ingredients such as fried bread croûtons or dumplings and stick to additions which are completely non-fattening. Finely chopped parsley, for instance, thin slices of lemon, thin slices of young leeks or spring onions, wafer thin slices of firm button mushrooms, added at the last minute, or some chopped hard-boiled egg white.

GARNISHES FOR COLD SOUPS

Cold soups should look cool and taste cool. Garnishes are important and can make all the difference to the look of the dish. Add thinly sliced, peeled cucumber to pale soups; thin slices of lemon to bright-coloured soups; a spoonful of well-chilled and seasoned sour cream to each serving of cold soups which need a lift, or thinly sliced radishes to soups which need a slight sharpening of flavour. Finely shredded lettuce, grated lemon or orange peel or a thin slice or two of avocado also make attractive garnishings.

HOME-MADE STOCKS FOR SOUPS AND SAUCES

Since so many firms started producing those useful little concentrated stock cubes for both beef and chicken stock, it has been something of a temptation to forget about stock-making and save the trouble by using the mass-produced products. I must admit I did this for a time until I realized that all my soups, gravies and sauces had a sameness about them which they didn't have when I used the base of a home-made stock.

So much goodness is lost by throwing away vegetable peelings, bones and cooked carcasses that it really is a waste and an extravagance not to keep your own stock pot – let alone the fact of missing those exciting mixtures of flavours.

Cook bones until lightly browned in a heavy saucepan without any extra fat, add vegetable peelings, tomato skin (these give a good colour), mushroom stalks or peelings, onion skins and even a few oddities like half a lemon and the peel of some cooking apples. Cover with water, season with salt and freshly ground black pepper and add a few mixed herbs. Bring to the boil, cover and simmer gently for at least three hours (this can be done in the oven).

Strain the stock, leave to cool, remove any fat from the surface and keep in a refrigerator until required.

If the stock is not strong enough for your purpose, a stock cube can be added to strengthen it (this will not destroy the home-made taste) or, alternatively, stir in a tablespoon of tomato puree.

If you wish to keep the stock for a few days, bring it back to the boil every second day but remember to let it get cool before returning it to the refrigerator.

Stock from a Cooked Chicken Carcass

A chicken carcass and remaining skin from a cooked chicken still have a lot of goodness and flavour in them. Break up the bones, add plenty of vegetables and you will end up with a useful and nourishing soup. The secret lies in slow, gentle cooking and in giving the stock a good stir every now and then to extract all the flavour from the bones.

1 chicken carcass
1 rasher bacon
1 onion
1 stick celery
4 tomatoes
1 carrot
A bouquet garni
3½ pints water
½ teaspoon salt
8 peppercorns

Break up chicken carcass and chop the bacon. Wash onion but leave on the brown skins and cut into quarters. Wash and roughly chop celery including leaves. Roughly chop tomatoes. Peel and chop carrot.

Put chicken bones and skin in a large heavy pan and brown quickly over a high heat for two minutes, stirring to prevent burning. Add remaining ingredients and bring to the boil then cover and simmer gently for 2½ – 3 hours, stirring the stock every now and then to bring out the flavour. Strain through a fine sieve and leave to cool. Leave in a refrigerator until the fat has risen to the surface and set firm then scrape off all the fat and use the stock for soups, casseroles, stews and sauces.

Note: The stock will keep for a week in a refrigerator but should be brought to the boil every other day for safety.

Chicken and Egg Soup

A warming tasty soup that is full of goodness. If home made chicken stock is on the lightly-flavoured side, add a chicken stock cube to give body but go easy on the salt when seasoning.

2 pints strong chicken stock
2 egg yolks
Juice 1 lemon
1 tablespoon finely-chopped parsley
Salt and pepper

Bring stock to the boil and season with salt and pepper. Beat egg yolks well with the lemon juice and blend in two tablespoons of the hot stock. Remove stock from the heat and whisk in the egg mixture. Add parsley and serve at once.

Chicken Soup with Eggs and Cheese

An even more satisfying soup than the one above. A boon to those who are hungry but also figure conscious.

2 pints strong chicken stock
4 egg yolks
4 oz finely grated Cheddar or Gruyère cheese
Salt and pepper

Bring the stock to the boil and season with salt and pepper. Beat egg yolks well. Mix in the cheese and two tablespoons of the hot stock. Blend this mixture into the stock and heat through, stirring continually, without boiling. Continue to stir until the cheese has melted and the soup has thickened.

Chicken Lemon Soup with Lettuce

A variation on the traditional Greek soup but without the rice and with the addition of some shredded lettuce in the last minutes of cooking.

2 pints strong chicken stock
2 medium eggs
Juice ½ lemon
Salt and freshly ground black pepper
1 small lettuce heart

Heat the stock and season with salt, if necessary, and with a generous grinding of black peppercorns. Beat the eggs until smooth and blend in the lemon juice. Very finely shred the lettuce. Gradually add 3 tablespoons of the stock to the eggs and lemon juice, beating well. Add the mixture to the remaining stock with the shredded lettuce and heat through, without boiling, stirring all the time.

Serve at once.

Cabbage and Onion Soup

A good vegetable soup, made with a home-brewed stock, can be just as delicious as the most expensive hors d'oeuvre served in a five-star restaurant. Often it is the most simple ingredients which give the best results and a typical example is this country-tasting concoction of cabbage, onion and stock with a garnish of finely chopped hard-boiled egg whites. Use the egg yolks as a garnish for another dish.

½ lb green cabbage
1 medium onion
1 hard-boiled egg
1 tablespoon olive oil
2 pints stock (or water and stock cubes)
Few drops Tabasco (optional)
Salt and freshly ground black pepper

Very finely shred the cabbage. Peel and finely chop the onion. Shell the hard-boiled egg, remove the yolk and finely chop the white. Heat the olive oil in a saucepan, add the onion and cook over a medium high heat for 3 minutes until the onion is soft but not brown. Add the cabbage and continue to cook for a further 5 minutes, stirring continually over a medium heat. Pour over the stock, season with salt and freshly ground black pepper and a few drops of Tabasco. Bring to the boil, cover and simmer for 15 minutes or until the cabbage is just tender.

Pour into soup bowls and garnish with the finely-chopped hard-boiled egg white before serving.

A Fine Soup of Mange-tout Peas

Mange-tout peas, or sugar peas as they are sometimes called, used to be a rarity in England and the only sure way of getting these deliciously tender peas, which are eaten whole in the pod, was to grow them oneself. Now, with the Common Market and a wider interest in unusual vegetables, the situation has changed. Mange-tout peas can be found in many good vegetable shops and, in fact, when I invented this recipe I bought some real beauties from the food department of Marks and Spencer.

This is a light, attractive-looking soup with a very subtle flavour. The thinly sliced peas give it an interesting texture.

½ lb mange-tout peas
1 onion
½ tablespoon olive oil
2 pints good chicken stock (or water and stock cubes)
Juice ½ lemon
Salt and pepper
2 egg yolks

Remove the tops and tails of the peas and cut them across into very thin slices. Peel and very finely chop the onion. Heat the olive oil in a saucepan, add the onion and cook over a medium low heat until the onion is soft and transparent. Add the peas and continue to cook for a further 2 minutes. Add the stock and lemon juice, season with salt and freshly ground black pepper, bring to the boil, cover and simmer gently for 15 minutes until the peas are tender but still have a slight crunch to them. Beat the egg yolks and blend in a little of the soup. Add the egg yolks to the soup and beat well to prevent them curdling. Heat through but *do not boil.*

Serve with celery stalks stuffed with cream cheese or cottage cheese and sprinkled with a little cayenne.

Mushroom and Avocado Soup

6 oz firm button mushrooms
½ tablespoon olive oil
2 pints chicken stock (or stock cubes and water)
2 egg yolks
2 tablespoons sour cream
Salt and freshly ground black pepper
2 tablespoons finely-chopped parsley
½ avocado

Thinly slice the mushrooms. Heat the olive oil, add the mushrooms and cook over a medium high heat for 4 minutes. Drain off excess olive oil, add the stock and bring to the boil. Season with salt and pepper and simmer gently for 10 minutes. Beat the egg yolks with the sour cream. Add a little of the soup and mix well. Add the egg yolk mixture to the rest of the soup and whisk in with a wire whisk over a low heat, without boiling. Season with salt and pepper and mix in the finely-chopped parsley.

Peel the avocado, cut into very thin slices, and add to the soup. Heat through without boiling, check seasoning and serve at once.

November Soup

The taste for celeriac (similar to celery but somehow more subtle) is one that should be more widespread. I have tried to grow it without any success and I have to rely on the imported roots which appear in the greengrocers during the Autumn months. In this clear vegetable soup celeriac gives the major flavour and although it could be said to be a basically simple, country soup, I feel it is worthy of being produced for the most sophisticated company.

½ lb celeriac root
1 large carrot
1 large onion
½ oz butter
1 small tin tomatoes
1½ pints stock (or water and stock cubes)
Salt and pepper
Small pinch mixed herbs

Peel off the hard outer skin of the celeriac and cut the root into very thin matchstick strips about half an inch long. Peel the carrot and cut into very small dice. Peel the onion and chop finely. Heat the butter in a heavy pan, add the vegetables and cook over a medium low heat until the onion is transparent and the vegetables are soft – about 4–5 minutes. Add the tomatoes and mix well. Pour over the stock, add the herbs and season with salt and pepper. Bring to the boil, cover and simmer gently for 45 minutes to bring out the flavour of all the vegetables. Mix well with a wire whisk to break up the tomatoes, check for seasoning and serve with hot salted biscuits or Melba toast.

Curried Celery and Apple Soup

2 cooking apples
1 medium onion
3 sticks celery
½ oz butter
2 pints stock
2 teaspoons curry powder
2 tablespoons sour cream
1 tablespoon finely-chopped celery leaves
Salt and pepper

Peel and slice apples. Peel and chop onion. Thinly slice celery. Melt butter in a saucepan, add apples and vegetables and cook over a medium heat, without browning, until onions are transparent. Mix in curry powder and stock. Bring to the boil, lower the heat and simmer gently for twenty to thirty minutes until apples and vegetables are tender. Purée the soup in an electric liquidizer, through a food mill or a fine sieve and return to a clean pan. Add cream, season with salt and pepper and heat through, without boiling.

Garnish with finely-chopped celery leaves.

May Soup

Hard-boiled eggs, chopped and lightly fried and added at the last minute give this economical soup an unusual flavour.

2 onions
3 old carrots
4 cauliflower leaves
1½ tablespoons olive oil
2½ pints water
2 tablespoons tomato purée
2 tablespoons finely-chopped parsley
Salt and pepper
2 hard-boiled eggs

Peel and finely chop onions. Peel and coarsely grate carrots. Finely shred cauliflower leaves. Heat 1 tablespoon oil in a large saucepan. Add vegetables and cook over a medium heat until onion is transparent. Add water, tomato purée and parsley, season with salt and pepper and bring to the boil. Lower the heat, cover the soup and simmer slowly for 40 minutes until all the vegetables are tender.

Chop hard boiled eggs and fry them in ½ tablespoon oil for 2 minutes over a medium heat. Add to the soup just before serving.

Hot Cucumber Soup

Cold cucumber soup is a popular starter in the summer. This hot cucumber soup is more unusual and now that cucumbers are usually available all the year round it makes a delicious first course at any time of the year.

1 cucumber
1 small onion
1 clove garlic
1 oz butter
2 pints strong chicken stock (or water and stock cubes)
1 tablespoon chopped parsley
½ teaspoon chervil
Salt and pepper
1 carton sour cream (5 fl oz)
2 oz Gruyère cheese

Cut the thin stem off the cucumber and finely grate the flesh and skin. Peel and finely chop the onion and garlic clove. Melt the butter in a saucepan, add the onion, garlic and cucumber and cook over a medium low heat for four minutes until the onion is soft. Pour over the stock, add the parsley and chervil, season with salt and pepper, bring to the boil and simmer for twenty minutes until the cucumber is soft. Purée the soup in an electric liquidizer, through a fine food mill or through a sieve. Check the seasoning, return to a clean pan and blend in the sour cream. Heat through without boiling and serve with very small cubes of Gruyère cheese as a garnish.

Serves 4–5

Iced Tomato and Celery Soup

- 4 sticks celery
- 1 clove garlic
- 2 pints tomato juice
- 2 teaspoons lemon juice
- Salt and freshly ground black pepper
- Pinch cayenne pepper
- 2 celery leaves

Grate the celery stalks and reserve all the juice. Crush the garlic. Combine the celery, tomato juice, lemon juice and garlic in a saucepan. Season with salt, pepper and a little cayenne, and cook over a low heat, without boiling, for 15 minutes. Strain, cool and chill in a refrigerator until icy cold.

Garnish the soup with finely-chopped celery leaves.

Jellied Cucumber Soup

A cool, cool starter for summer evenings.

- 1 cucumber
- 1 teaspoon finely-chopped mint
- ½ tablespoon lemon juice
- 1 tablespoon finely-grated onion
- 1 tin consommé
- Salt and pepper
- 2 oz peeled prawns for garnishing

Peel the cucumber and grate the flesh through a fairly coarse grater. Soak the mint leaves in lemon juice for 10 minutes. Add the cucumber, onion, mint and lemon juice to the consommé and mix well. Season with salt and pepper and pour into four soup bowls or cups. Chill in a refrigerator until set and garnish with the prawns before serving.

Iced Tomato and Orange Soup

2 lb ripe tomatoes
1 onion
2 cloves garlic
1 teaspoon paprika pepper
2 tablespoons red wine
Juice and grated rind 1 orange
8 black olives

Peel the tomatoes (see page xii). Peel the onion. Put the tomato and onion through the fine blades of a mincing machine. Crush the garlic and mix with the paprika. Add the garlic and paprika to the tomatoes and onion and mix in the red wine, orange juice and rind. Season with salt and pepper and stir well. Chill the soup in the refrigerator for at least two hours and garnish with thin slivers of black olives.

Gazpacho

This famous Spanish soup, made with a strong flavouring of garlic and blended cucumber and tomatoes is usually made with a base of white bread. In this recipe, I substitute egg yolks for the bread crumbs in order to make the original emulsified mixture.

3–4 cloves garlic
2 egg yolks
¼ pint olive oil
1 onion
1 cucumber
1 lb ripe tomatoes
1 green pepper
Salt and freshly ground black pepper

Crush the garlic cloves with a little salt and pepper, add the yolks and beat until smooth. Gradually blend in the olive oil, a few drops at a time, stirring continually until each addition of oil has been absorbed into the egg yolks. Peel and grate the onion. Grate the cucumber with the skin. Peel the tomatoes (see page xii) and remove the seeds. Remove the core and seeds of the pepper and pass the tomatoes and pepper through the coarse blades of a mincing machine. Add the onion, cucumber, tomatoes and pepper to the mayonnaise base and mix well. Season with salt and pepper and add a little cold water if the consistency is too thick. Chill in a refrigerator and serve icy cold.

Pink Prawn Soup

4 cartons yoghurt (20 fl oz)
1 pint tomato juice
Juice ½ lemon
Salt and pepper
Pinch cayenne pepper
1 small cucumber
6 oz peeled prawns
2 tablespoons finely-chopped chives

Combine the yoghurt and tomato juice and whisk to blend. Add the lemon juice and seasoning. Remove the peel of the cucumber, coarsely grate the flesh, sprinkle it with salt and leave to stand for twenty minutes. Drain off the excess liquid and add the cucumber to the soup with the prawns. Chill in a refrigerator and serve really cold with a garnish of chopped chives.

Copacabana Turtle Soup

A quick soup to serve either hot or cold (conservationists will be relieved to know that turtles are now being farmed successfully).

2 tins John Lusty turtle soup
1 teaspoon lemon juice
1 tablespoon sherry
Pinch salt and a little freshly ground black pepper
1 firm but ripe avocado

To serve hot:

Strain the soup into a saucepan and add the pieces of turtle, cut into very thin slivers. Add the lemon juice and sherry and season with a little salt and freshly ground black pepper. Peel and halve the avocado and cut into thin slices. Add the avocado to the soup and serve at once.

To serve chilled:

Strain the soup and chop the turtle pieces into thin slivers and add to the soup. Add the lemon juice and sherry and season with a little salt and freshly ground black pepper. Pour into 4 soup bowls.

Peel and halve the avocado and cut the flesh into very thin slices, divide these between the four servings and chill in a refrigerator for at least 2 hours before serving.

Tomato and Fish Soup

This is a hearty soup which need only be followed by a light main course such as an omelet or cheese soufflé.

1 lb tomatoes
2 onions
2 pints water
1 teaspoon lemon juice
Salt and pepper
1 lb cod, hake or halibut
1 bunch watercress

Peel and chop the tomatoes. Peel and chop the onions. Combine the tomatoes, onions and water in a saucepan with the lemon juice, season with salt and pepper, bring to the boil and simmer for 20 minutes. Cut the fish into small cubes. Remove the tough stalks of the watercress and chop the leaves. Add the fish and watercress to the soup and cook for a further 10 minutes or until the fish is just tender. Check seasoning and serve at once.

Curried Turtle Soup

2 tins John Lusty's turtle soup
1 teaspoon curry powder
1 teaspoon lemon juice
2 teaspoons tomato purée
4 tablespoons sour cream

Strain the soup into a saucepan and reserve the turtle meat. Add the curry powder, lemon juice and tomato purée to the soup, heat through and simmer for 5 minutes. Very thinly slice the turtle meat and add it to the soup. Pour into soup bowls and top each serving with a spoonful of sour cream at the last minute.

Avocado and Cucumber Soup

2 ripe avocados
Juice ½ lemon
½ cucumber
1½ pints milk
1 beef stock cube dissolved in 2 tablespoons boiling water
1 teaspoon grated onion
3 tablespoons sour cream or yoghurt
1 tablespoon chopped chives
Salt and pepper

Peel avocados and remove stones. Sprinkle at once with lemon juice. Combine avocados, cucumber (peeled and cut into small pieces) and milk and purée through a fine food mill or in an electric liquidizer. Add stock cube and water. Add onion, blend in cream or yoghurt and season with salt and pepper. Chill well and serve cold with a sprinkling of chopped chives on each portion.

Iced Cucumber Soup

A cool, refreshing soup with the luxury addition of some pink prawns.

2 large cucumbers
1 shallot
2 teaspoons lemon juice
1 tin consommé
1 teaspoon finely-chopped mint
2 oz peeled prawns

Grate the cucumbers through a medium grater. Grate the peeled shallot through a fine grater. Combine the cucumber, shallot and lemon juice and season with salt and pepper. Mix in the consommé and the mint and pour into four soup cups or bowls. Refrigerate for at least 2 hours and garnish with peeled prawns.

Balanced first courses which keep a check on the calorie count

THE FIRST COURSE

The first course or starter should be a light dish, an appetizer and a contrast to the main course. For the weight-conscious, the first course can be a danger; rich dishes with cream sauces should be avoided, so should food which is served in pastry cases or on toast. Deep fried ingredients should also be avoided as should very highly seasoned foods which excite the appetite too much and tend to encourage one to over-indulge in the main course.

All that sounds a bit depressing but in fact the first course provides ample scope for the weight-watcher. Cold dishes tend, on the whole to be less fattening than those which are to be served hot: there is a vast variety of light hot and cold soups, egg, fish and vegetable dishes which make delicious first courses and any number of non-fattening hors d'oeuvres.

The first course sets the tone of the whole meal; it should be attractive to look at and, if the dish is to be served cold, it should be really well chilled. Take care with the garnishing of all dishes and remember that little things like a sprinkling of freshly chopped parsley or chives, some thin slices of lemon or a border of cool, wafer-thin cucumber slices can make all the difference to the appearance and enjoyment of a dish.

The balance of the first course to the main course is also important. If the first course is light it can be followed by a substantial main course. If, on the other hand, the first course is to be made from fairly rich ingredients care must be taken to plan a light main course.

Most first courses, especially if they are cold, can be made in advance, a factor which is of importance to the busy cook, but remember that if the dishes are to be served hot and you wish to cook them in advance for re-heating at the last minute do allow for the re-heating time and avoid over-cooking the ingredients – over-cooking spoils both the texture of the food and its taste.

Plan meals in advance so that a good contrast of both taste, texture and colour is obtained between the first and the main courses.

ACCOMPANIMENTS TO FIRST COURSES

If you care about calories then it is obviously not a good idea to accompany the first course with great chunks of French bread dripping with garlic butter, to serve a soup with bowls of fried bread croûtons or to supply generously buttered brown bread with fish dishes. Ideally the first course should be able to stand up on its own without any starch on the side but if you do feel the need for something extra then why not serve Melba toast (thin slices of bread toasted, split and baked in a hot oven until crisp and slightly curled) or some stalks of celery stuffed with cottage cheese.

In place of the fried bread croûtons, try serving some tiny cubes of Cheddar or Gruyère cheese with a hot soup; these are really delicious and add an exotic taste.

With cold soups serve small bowls of finely chopped chives, chopped tomatoes, thin slices of radishes or wafer thin slices of lemon to float on the surface.

Tomato Juice Cocktail

Tomato juice as a first course always evokes rather dismal memories for me of railway meals or second-rate hotels when the alternatives are 'fruit juice' or 'grapefruit segments' both served straight from their tins and unpleasantly warm.

A well seasoned and spiced tomato juice cocktail served icy cold in a frosted glass, on the other hand, can be really delicious if a little time and trouble is taken with it.

1 tin tomato juice
Juice ½ lemon
½ tablespoon very finely-chopped chives or 1 teaspoon grated raw onion
½ teaspoon Worcestershire sauce
Few drops Tabasco sauce
Celery salt and freshly ground black pepper
Thin slices of lemon to garnish

Combine the tomato juice, lemon juice, chives or onion, Worcestershire and Tabasco sauces, season with celery salt and pepper and mix together very well (preferably in a shaker or screw top jar). Chill in a refrigerator for at least half an hour and serve in glasses or goblets which have also been chilled in a refrigerator for a time. Float a slice of lemon on the surface of each glass. Serve well chilled with salted biscuits.

Stibelesh

A rather exotic and very 'cool' starter of yoghurt, sour cream, finely chopped vegetables and chopped prawns. Serve it when you want to make an impression with an unusual dish.

4 tomatoes
1 red pepper
4 spring onions
1 clove garlic
1 carton yoghurt (5 fl oz)
1 carton sour cream (5 fl oz)
1 teaspoon lemon juice
Few drops Tabasco sauce
Salt and freshly ground black pepper
4 oz peeled prawns
4 finely-chopped mint leaves

Peel the tomatoes (see page xii), remove the seeds and finely chop the flesh. Remove the core and seeds from the pepper and finely chop the flesh. Very thinly slice the spring onions. Squeeze the garlic through a garlic press and roughly chop the prawns. Combine the yoghurt with the sour cream and beat until smooth. Add the tomatoes, red peppers, spring onions, garlic and Tabasco. Season with salt and pepper and fold in the prawns and finely-chopped mint. Spoon into four serving dishes and chill for at least 30 minutes in a refrigerator before serving.

Cottage Cheese Custard

An unusual first course which looks attractive and has a subtle flavour. Make it in individual ramekin dishes and serve as soon as it is cooked.

4 eggs
½ lb cottage cheese
¼ pint thin cream
Salt and pepper
Pinch cayenne pepper

Separate the eggs. Beat the yolks lightly to break them up and combine them with the cottage cheese and cream. Season with salt, pepper and a pinch of cayenne. Beat the egg whites until stiff and fold them into the soufflé base. Turn into 4 lightly-greased ramekin dishes. Place the dishes in a baking tin half filled with hot water and bake in a very moderate oven (350° F, Reg 4) for about 30 minutes or until set. Serve at once.

Tomato and Anchovy Salad

The drawback of anchovies is their saltiness; avoid this by soaking the fillets in a little milk before using; the milk draws off the salt but does not impair the flavour.

½ lb firm ripe tomatoes (the large continental ones are ideal if you can find them)
6 anchovy fillets
Milk
3 hard-boiled eggs
1 small onion
1 tablespoon capers

Dressing

Juice 1 lemon
2 tablespoons tomato ketchup
Salt and freshly ground black pepper

Soak the anchovies in a little milk, squeeze out the liquid and pat the anchovies dry with kitchen paper. Peel the tomatoes (see page xii) if they are the English kind; leave continental tomatoes unpeeled. Cut the tomatoes into thin slices. Cut the anchovies into half lengthways. Slice the hard-boiled eggs. Peel the onion, cut it into wafer-thin slices and divide into rings.

Arrange the tomatoes, egg slices and onion rings in a shallow serving dish and top with a lattice pattern of anchovy fillets. Scatter over the capers and pour over a dressing made by combining the lemon juice and tomato ketchup well seasoned with salt and pepper. Chill before serving.

Fonds d'Artichauts and Prawn Salad

Tinned artichoke bottoms can be obtained from most delicatessen shops and make a good combination with prawns in a first course which goes well before a substantial main dish.

1 tin fonds d'artichauts
2 tomatoes
6 small clove garlic
1 oz peeled prawns
1 tablespoon finely-chopped chives or spring onion tops
3 tablespoons olive oil
1 tablespoon white wine vinegar
Salt and freshly ground black pepper

Drain the liquid from the fonds d'artichauts and cut them into thin slices. Peel the tomatoes (see page xii), remove the core and seeds and roughly chop the flesh. Crush the garlic or press it through a garlic press. Combine the prawns, fonds d'artichauts, tomatoes and chives or spring onion tops in a bowl. Combine the garlic, oil and vinegar in a screw-top jar, season with salt and freshly ground black pepper, put on the top, and shake well. Pour the dressing over the salad, toss lightly and chill in a refrigerator for at least two hours. Serve in glass goblets.

Globe Artichokes with Marinated Prawns

4 globe artichokes
2 cloves garlic
1 ripe tomato
$\frac{1}{4}$ lb peeled prawns
3 tablespoons olive oil
1 tablespoon white wine vinegar
1 teaspoon French Dijon mustard
Salt and freshly ground black pepper
1 tablespoon very finely-chopped parsley

Using a pair of kitchen scissors, cut half an inch off the pointed tops of the artichoke leaves. Peel the garlic, chop very finely and stuff deep between the leaves. Place the artichokes upside down in a large pan with two inches of boiling, salted water. Cover tightly and simmer gently for 20–30 minutes. Test [illegible] a sharp pointed knife to see if the bases of the artichokes [illegible] tender. Drain the artichokes upside down in a colander [illegible] leave to cool. Peel the tomato, discard the seeds and finely chop the flesh. Chop the peeled prawns. Combine the olive oil, vinegar and mustard in a screw-top jar and shake to mix well. Mix in the chopped tomato, parsley and prawns and season with salt and pepper. Remove the centre small leaves of the artichokes and pull the chokes (the tough, hairy fibres) from the bases. Fill the centres with the prawn dressing and chill in a refrigerator for at least 30 minutes before serving.

AVOCADOS

Avocados are rich in fat and calories so they don't really make the most ideal of non-fattening first courses. On the other hand, the fruit is rich also in vitamins and proteins and provided it is followed by a sensible main course and not served with too rich a sauce or filling, I feel it would be sad to ignore them in this collection of recipes.

Buying avocados in this country can be a problem. They have, of necessity, to be imported while under-ripe and, unfortunately, most greengrocers don't seem to take the trouble to learn how to tell their condition, and advise the buyer on it. I find it safest to buy firm, hard fruit, place them in a sealed brown paper bag and leave them to ripen in a warm place for 3–4 days until the flesh gives to the touch.

Avocados with Cottage Cheese

4 spring onions
1 clove garlic
½ lb cottage cheese
1 tablespoon lemon juice
2 medium avocados
Salt
Paprika pepper

Trim and finely chop the spring onions and peel and crush the garlic or press it through a garlic press. Mix the onions and garlic into the cottage cheese with one teaspoon lemon juice and season with salt. Halve the avocados, remove the stones and sprinkle the flesh with the remaining lemon juice to prevent browning. Fill the cavities with the cheese mixture and dust the top with a little paprika pepper. Serve chilled.

Avocados with Prawns and Sour Cream

A fresh tasting and refreshing first course for the summer – serve it well chilled.

3 teaspoons lemon juice
1 carton sour cream (5 fl oz)
Salt and freshly ground black pepper
Few drops Tabasco sauce
4 oz peeled prawns
2 medium avocados
1 teaspoon finely-chopped chives

Add 1 teaspoon lemon juice to the sour cream and mix well. Season with salt, pepper and a few drops of Tabasco and fold in the prawns. Halve the avocados, remove the stones and sprinkle the remaining lemon juice over the surface to prevent browning. Fill the cavities with the prawn mixture, sprinkle over the chives and chill before serving.

Melon and Grape Salad

I discovered this simple, refreshing first course in that fabulous restaurant, Odins. It makes an excellent start to a meal which has a rather rich main course.

1 small melon
½ lb black grapes
1 small sprig of mint
3 tablespoons olive oil
1 tablespoon white wine vinegar
Salt and freshly ground black pepper

Remove the peel and seeds of the melon and cut the flesh into cubes or balls. Halve the grapes and remove the seeds (if the skins are tough, remove those too – an unpleasant job but worth the effort). Very finely chop the mint. Combine the olive oil, vinegar and seasoning and mix well. Pour the dressing over the fruit and mint, toss lightly and chill for at least 2 hours before serving.

Mousse of Chicken Livers and Ham

Some dishes require a little hard work to make them into masterpieces and this is one of those dishes. Its secret lies in pounding the chicken livers and ham until they are really smooth and then whipping them with melted butter until the consistency resembles beaten cream. The result is worth working for. Serve with thick, freshly-made slices of white toasted bread.

6 oz chicken livers
2 oz ham
1 shallot
3 oz butter
1 dessertspoon brandy
1 clove garlic
Pinch thyme
Pinch tarragon
Salt and pepper
1 carton double cream (5 fl oz)
1 egg white

Remove tough membrane and any greenish-tinged parts of the chicken livers. Finely mince ham. Peel and finely chop shallot. Melt 1 oz butter in a heavy pan. Add onions and chicken livers and cook over a medium heat for two minutes. Add ham and continue cooking for a further two minutes (the liver should still be rosy pink on the inside). Place chicken livers and ham in a pestle and mortar. Pour over the brandy add garlic clove pressed through a garlic press and pound until the meat is smooth.

Melt remaining butter, add herbs and leave to cool but not stiffen. Whisk the butter with a wire whisk into the meat until the mixture is smooth and light. Season with salt and pepper.

Beat cream until stiff. Beat egg white until stiff but not dry. Fold cream and egg white into the meat and butter with a wooden spatula until well blended. Pile the mousse into an earthenware dish or on to a serving dish and chill until set firm. Garnish with cubes of aspic jelly (see page 200).

Serves 4–6

Egg and Anchovy Mousse

Some people make egg mousses in an electric liquidizer; this, I think, is a mistake as the resulting mixture is too smooth and bland. I like mine to have a slightly rougher texture with something to get one's teeth into.

However you make it, an egg mousse is an inexpensive and easily-made dish which can be served as a first or main course.

1 tin consommé
½ packet (¼ oz) gelatine
½ tablespoon lemon juice
1 tablespoon warm water
¼ pint tomato juice
1 tablespoon tomato purée
Pinch oregano or chervil
1 clove garlic
4 hard-boiled eggs
1 carton yoghurt (5 fl oz)
4 anchovy fillets
Freshly ground black pepper
1 egg white
1 tablespoon sherry
Few drops Tabasco sauce

Reserve ¼ pint of consommé. Soften the gelatine in the lemon juice and 1 tablespoon warm water. Combine the remaining consommé, tomato juice, tomato purée, herbs and the garlic pressed through a garlic press, in a saucepan and simmer gently for 5 minutes. Mix in the gelatine and leave until cold and beginning to thicken. Chop the hard-boiled eggs and mix them with the yoghurt. Finely chop the anchovy fillets and add them to the egg mixture. Season with freshly ground black pepper and a few drops of Tabasco sauce.

Whip the egg white until stiff. Fold the egg mixture and egg white into the setting jelly and turn into a glass dish. Leave in a refrigerator until set. Combine ¼ pint consommé with the sherry and pour it over the mousse. Return to the refrigerator for ½ hour until the consommé has set.

Serve as a first course or with salad as a main course.

Stuffed Anchovy Eggs

8 eggs
1 tin anchovies
2 tablespoons tomato ketchup
2 tablespoons sour cream
Salt and pepper
1 oz butter
1 oz flour
¼ pint milk
1 carton yoghurt (5 fl oz)
2 oz grated Gruyère cheese
½ teaspoon paprika pepper

Hard boil eggs for 8 minutes in boiling water. Rinse under cold running water; remove shells and halve eggs lengthways. Scoop out yolks into a bowl. Drain excess oil off anchovies and mash the fillets pounding them into a smooth paste. Blend in tomato ketchup and 2 tablespoons sour cream and season with salt and pepper. Fill the egg whites with this mixture and arrange them, cut sides down, in a shallow baking dish.

Melt butter in a saucepan. Add flour and mix well. Gradually blend in milk, stirring continually over a medium heat until the sauce is smooth and very thick. Remove from the heat. Beat in yoghurt and half the Gruyère cheese and season with salt and pepper. Pour the sauce over the eggs. Top with remaining cheese and sprinkle with a little paprika pepper. Cook under a hot grill for a few minutes until eggs are hot through and the surface is golden brown.

Egg and Avocado Mayonnaise

An unusual way of serving an egg mayonnaise; follow with a fairly light main course.

6 hard-boiled eggs
½ ripe avocado
Juice ½ lemon
6 tablespoons olive oil
Salt and pepper
1 tablespoon chopped spring onion tops
1 lettuce

Shell the eggs and cut them in half lengthways. Arrange the halves, flat side down, on a bed of lettuce leaves. Peel the avocado and mash the flesh with the lemon juice until smooth. Beat in the olive oil, a little at a time, until the mixture has emulsified and is thick and smooth. Season with salt and pepper, fold in the chopped onion tops and spread the avocado mayonnaise over the eggs. Chill before serving.

Lobster Cocktail

Lobsters, sadly, are prohibitively expensive and, due to the heavy over-fishing of these shellfish every year, they continue to get more and more pricey. I am violently against most types of factory farming but I do think there will be something to be said for a successful venture to farm lobsters, even if it is only to replenish the sea beds.

Here is an exotic first course which sets a luxury tone to the whole meal. Lobster is a rich fish and this starter should be followed by a light main course.

1 lobster
2 lettuce hearts
1½ cartons sour cream (7½ fl oz)
2 tablespoons tomato ketchup
A few drops of Tabasco sauce
¼ teaspoon Worcestershire sauce
Salt and freshly ground black pepper
½ lemon
Pinch cayenne pepper

Split the lobster down the back, remove the stomach and thin line of black intestine. Crush the claws, remove the meat and remove all the meat from the tail (the shell and head can be boiled to make stock for a lobster soup). Cut the meat into ½ inch pieces. Finely shred the lettuce and arrange it in the bottom of 4 glass goblets. Divide the lobster meat into four and place the pieces on top of the lettuce. Combine the sour cream, tomato ketchup and Worcestershire sauce and mix well. Season with salt and pepper and pour the dressing over the lobster. Top with a tiny sprinkling of cayenne and with a thin slice of lemon. Chill before serving.

Smoked Mackerel

Smoked fish is always popular as a first course and, to my mind smoked mackerel (a fairly new innovation), is on a par with smoked trout, smoked eel and even most smoked salmon; yet it costs a quarter of the price. Serve it *au naturel* as a first course with very, very thin slices of brown bread and butter.

4 small smoked mackerel
1 lettuce heart
1½ lemons
6 tablespoons horseradish sauce
1 tablespoon sour cream

Remove the skin from the mackerel and arrange the fish on lettuce leaves on four plates. Garnish with thin slices of lemon cut from the ½ lemon and serve with the horseradish sauce blended with the sour cream and quarters of lemon. Chill before serving.

Smoked Mackerel with Scrambled Eggs

Both smoked salmon and smoked eel with scrambled eggs are well tried Scandinavian recipes which make sumptuous luncheon or supper dishes – but at a price! Smoked mackerel is equally delicious and far cheaper than the more well-known smoked fish. This recipe is one I would be proud to serve to any company and the only drawback it has is that the eggs must be made immediately before being eaten, or they lose that shiny, smooth texture which is so important.

2 medium smoked mackerel
1 teaspoon lemon juice
6 eggs
1 tablespoon top of milk
(or thin cream)
1 oz butter
Salt and pepper

Remove the skin from the mackerel and slide the fillets off the bone in eight neat sections. Arrange the fillets around the edge of a serving dish and sprinkle the fish with lemon juice. Beat the eggs lightly with a fork, blend in the milk or cream and season with salt and pepper. Melt the butter in a heavy pan or non-stick saucepan, add the eggs and cook over a very low heat, stirring occasionally until the eggs are just set. Spoon the egg immediately into the centre of the serving dish and serve at once with brown bread and butter or hot toast. The dish can be garnished with sprigs of fresh parsley.

Cucumber and Cream Cheese Ring

This is a cool and attractive summer dish which is quick and easy to make and which can act as the basis for a variety of different and exciting dishes.

1 cucumber
8 oz cream cheese
Juice 1 lemon
2 tablespoons water
1 packet (1 tablespoon) gelatine
1 small onion
Salt and pepper
Cayenne pepper

Coarsely grate the cucumber. Mash the cream cheese and blend in the cucumber. Combine the lemon juice and water, blend in the gelatine and heat gently until the gelatine is melted. Cool and add to the cucumber and cheese mixture and mix well. Very finely grate the onion and add it to the cucumber mixture. Season with salt, pepper and a pinch of cayenne and pour into a ring mould. Chill in a refrigerator for at least two hours, or until set. Turn out and serve with any of the following:

SMOKED MACKEREL AND HORSERADISH SAUCE

1 cucumber and cream cheese ring as above
2 small smoked mackerel
2 lemons
2 tablespoons made horseradish sauce
1 carton sour cream (5 fl oz)
1 tablespoon finely-chopped chives
Salt and pepper

Skin the mackerel and neatly detach the fillets. Divide each fillet into two and arrange them around the outside of the cucumber and cream cheese ring. Garnish with quarters of lemon. Combine the horseradish sauce, sour cream and chives, season with salt and pepper and mix well. Spoon the sauce into the centre of the ring, chill well before serving and serve with Melba toast or very thin slices of brown bread and butter.

TOMATO SALAD

1 cucumber and cream cheese ring as above
1 lb tomatoes
3 tablespoons olive oil
1 tablespoon white wine vinegar
1 teaspoon mustard
Salt and freshly ground black pepper
1 tablespoon finely-chopped chives or fresh basil leaves

Peel the tomatoes (see page xii). Remove the core and seeds

and finely chop the flesh. Combine the olive oil, vinegar and mustard in a screw-top jar, season with salt and pepper and shake well. Pour over the tomatoes and toss the salad lightly. Spoon the tomatoes into the centre and round the sides of the cucumber and cream cheese ring. Chill before serving.

PRAWN AND AVOCADO

1 cucumber and cream cheese ring as above
3 tablespoons olive oil
1 tablespoon white wine vinegar
1 teaspoon mustard
Salt and pepper
1 avocado
6 oz peeled prawns

Combine the olive oil, vinegar and mustard in a screw-top jar. Season with salt and pepper and shake to mix well. Peel the avocado, cut in half, remove the stone and cut into thin slices. Combine the avocado and prawns in a bowl, pour over the dressing and toss lightly. Fill the centre of the cucumber and cream cheese ring with the avocado and prawns and chill well before serving.

Cabilla Starter

An exciting first course which only takes minutes to make and virtually no cooking at all.

1 medium smoked mackerel
2 hard-boiled eggs
1 tablespoon finely-chopped chives
1 teaspoon made horseradish sauce
1 carton sour cream (5 fl oz)
Freshly ground black pepper
A little cayenne pepper

Remove the skin from the smoked mackerel, slide the fillets

off the bone and flake the flesh gently with a fork. Peel and chop the hard-boiled eggs. Fold the mackerel, eggs, horseradish sauce and chives into the sour cream with a seasoning of freshly ground black pepper and spoon the mixture into four small ramekin dishes. Sprinkle the top with a tiny pinch of cayenne. Serve with hot salted biscuits, cream crackers or freshly-made toast.

Dressed Crab a la Vinaigrette

Dressed crab is one of the most delicious of shellfish (although torture to prepare oneself) but it can be too rich for many people when it is served with a mayonnaise accompaniment. Sharper and more in contrast to the blandness of the brown meat of the crab is a vinaigrette sauce with the addition of finely-chopped chives, parsley and a hint of capers.

4 small dressed crabs in the shell
6 tablespoons olive oil
2 tablespoons white wine vinegar
¼ teaspoon French Dijon mustard
½ tablespoon very finely-chopped chives
½ tablespoon very finely-chopped parsley
½ teaspoon very finely-chopped capers
Salt and freshly ground black pepper

Combine all the ingredients for the dressing in a screw-top jar, season with salt and pepper, put on the top and shake really well until all the ingredients are well amalgamated. Leave in a refrigerator for the flavours to mature for 1 hour and then pour over the dressed crab. Serve chilled with very thin slices of buttered brown bread.

AN ALTERNATIVE DRESSING FOR DRESSED CRAB

Less rich than a traditional mayonnaise but with more body than the vinaigrette above, this sauce makes a good dressing for crab which is to be served as a substantial main course.

- 4 medium to large dressed crabs
- 1 carton sour cream (5 fl oz)
- 1 tablespoon tomato ketchup
- Few drops Worcestershire sauce
- 1 tablespoon very finely-chopped mixed pickles

Combine all the ingredients, mix well, check seasoning and pour over the dressed crabs. Serve with a salad on the side.

Smoked Salmon Dreams

An unusual and exciting first course which really tastes as delicious as it looks. The chopped walnuts give an interesting crunchy texture to the cottage cheese filling.

- 4 oz cottage cheese
- ½ teaspoon lemon juice
- Freshly ground black pepper
- Pinch paprika pepper
- Few drops Tabasco sauce
- 2 oz chopped walnuts
- 4 oz smoked salmon cut in wafer-thin slices
- Finely shredded lettuce
- Quarters of lemon

Blend cream cheese with lemon juice and season with freshly ground black pepper, paprika and Tabasco sauce. Mix in the chopped walnuts. Spread some of the cheese mixture on to each slice of smoked salmon and roll up neatly. Arrange salmon rolls on a bed of finely-shredded lettuce and garnish with quarters of lemon.

Tarama Salata with Prawns

2 oz smoked cod's roe
4 oz white bread
1 clove garlic
Juice ½ lemon
¼ pint olive oil
2 tablespoons yoghurt
Freshly ground black pepper
1 tablespoon chopped chives
2 oz peeled prawns
Melba toast

Remove crusts and soak bread in warm water until soft. Squeeze out excess water. Combine bread with cod's roe and pound or mash until really smooth. Squeeze garlic through a garlic press and add to cod's roe with lemon juice. Mix well. Gradually add olive oil, drop by drop (as for mayonnaise) until each drop of oil is absorbed into the cod's roe. When all the oil is used up, blend in the yoghurt, season with black pepper and mix in chives. Chop the prawns and add them to the tarama salata. Pack into a jar or small earthenware dish and chill for at least one hour before serving.

Serve with Melba toast and accompany with matchstick lengths of celery and red peppers, and with some plump black olives.

Broad Bean Starter

All too often the fresh nutty taste of young broad beans is lost through overcooking. In this recipe young beans are cooked until just tender, then skinned and combined with eggs, anchovies and tomatoes to make an appetizing summer starter.

8 oz shelled young broad beans
3 ripe tomatoes
3 hard-boiled eggs
1 small tin anchovy fillets
1 tablespoon finely-chopped chives
¼ pint vinaigrette dressing

Cook beans in boiling salted water until just tender. Drain, cool and remove the skins. Peel and thinly slice tomatoes, Shell and slice eggs. Drain off excess oil from anchovy fillets and divide each fillet in half down the centre. Arrange alternate layers of tomatoes, eggs and beans in a shallow serving dish. Criss-cross the surface with a pattern of anchovy fillets and sprinkle over the finely chopped chives. Pour over the vinaigrette dressing and chill before serving.

Light and delicate fish dishes to serve at any time of the year

Poached Salmon, Sea Trout or Trout, to Serve Cold

The timing of these delicately fleshed fish is always tricky however hard you work out the cooking time per pound. Luckily, there is a foolproof method which cooks any salmon, sea trout or trout to perfection, whatever the weight or size. It should really be described as coddling rather than poaching as the fish is removed from the heat as soon as the liquid boils.

Place the cleaned and gutted fish in a shallow container and cover it with water. Measure the water and to each pint add the following ingredients:

¼ pint dry white wine
2 tablespoons white wine vinegar
1 onion, peeled and sliced
1 small bay leaf
2 sprigs parsley
Pinch thyme
¼ teaspoon salt
6 peppercorns
1 tablespoon olive oil

Place the water and above ingredients in a saucepan, bring to the boil and simmer for 30–45 minutes. Strain and leave to stand until completely cold.

TO COOK THE FISH

Place the fish in a shallow pan. Pour over the liquid and bring to the boil over a *low* heat (this should take about ten minutes for a small fish). As soon as the liquid begins to bubble, remove the pan from the heat, cover it and leave it in a cool place until completely cold.

Jellied Trout

4 trout (8–12 ounces each), cooked as above
1 lemon
Horseradish sauce

Cook the trout as above and leave them to get cold in the cooking liquid. Carefully lift out the trout and arrange them in a shallow serving dish. Reheat the cooking liquid in a saucepan. Bring to the boil and cook over a high flame until the liquid has reduced to half. Strain through a muslin cloth, leave to cool and then pour over the fish. Place the dish in a refrigerator and leave for at least two hours for the liquid to become a firm jelly.

Serve chilled with wedges of lemon and horseradish sauce.

Cold Salmon or Sea Trout with Sauce Vert

Allow ½ lb fish on the bone for each serving.

1 salmon or sea trout cooked as above
½ cucumber
¾ pint mayonnaise (see page 194)
1 tablespoon finely-minced chives
3 tablespoons finely-chopped fresh tarragon leaves (or 1 tablespoon dried)
2 tablespoons very finely-chopped parsley
2 teaspoons very finely-chopped fresh dill (or ½ teaspoon dried)

(If the herbs used are dried, they should be soaked in 1 teaspoon of lemon juice and 1 tablespoon warm water for half an hour before using to bring out the flavour and soften them)

Remove the cold salmon or sea trout from the cooking liquid and carefully remove the skin and back fin – leave on the head and tail. Arrange the fish on a flat serving dish. Peel and very thinly slice the cucumber, sprinkle the slices with salt and leave them to 'sweat' for half an hour. Drain the slices well and pat them dry on kitchen paper. Garnish the fish with cucumber slices and chill in the refrigerator until required. Fold the finely-chopped herbs into the mayonnaise, check the seasoning and serve with the fish.

Salmon Mousse

- ½ oz (1 tablespoon) gelatine
- 2 tablespoons warm water
- 1 tablespoon lemon juice
- 1 teaspoon French Dijon mustard
- 2 tablespoons white wine vinegar
- 1 lb cooked salmon, flaked
- 3 sticks celery
- 2 teaspoons capers
- 1 carton sour cream (5 fl oz)
- 1 egg white
- Watercress
- Vinaigrette dressing (see page 191)

Combine the gelatine, water and lemon juice in a small saucepan and heat gently until gelatine is dissolved. Very finely chop the celery and the capers. Add the vinegar and mustard to the gelatine mixture and lightly mix in the fish, celery and capers. Beat the sour cream until light. Beat the egg white until stiff. Fold the cream and egg white into the fish and turn into a ring mould. Chill in a refrigerator for at least three hours, then turn out and fill the centre with sprigs of watercress dipped in vinaigrette dressing.

WHAT TO DO WITH SMALL QUANTITIES OF LEFTOVER COOKED SALMON

Salmon is a rich fish, besides having the best taste of any fish that swims the oceans or rivers of the world, and a little goes a long way. Whether you are given a fish, catch it yourself or buy it when prices are at their seasonal lowest, the chances are that there will be some left over. It may be only a *little* but in the case of salmon it can be put to good use in a number of ways to make interesting dishes.

Salmon and Sour Cream Omelet

6 eggs
1 tablespoon cold water
6 oz cooked salmon, flaked
½ tablespoon grated raw onion
½ carton sour cream (2½ fl oz)
Salt and freshly ground black pepper
½ oz butter

Beat the eggs lightly with a fork to break up the whites and yolks and blend in the water. Season the eggs lightly with salt and pepper. Fold the flaked salmon and grated onion into the sour cream and season with salt and freshly ground black pepper. Melt the butter in an omelet pan, add the eggs and cook over a medium heat, scoring the eggs through with a knife from time to time to spread the heat, until they are just beginning to set. Spread the salmon mixture along the centre of the omelet, cover and cook for a further minute to heat through and turn out on to a heated serving dish, folding the omelet neatly over. Serve at once.

Soused Salmon

Salmon should never be overcooked. Perfect poached salmon will only just come from the bone and the flesh should be moist and firm, not dry and flaking. Using a fish slice, slide the fish neatly off the centre bone and divide into serving portions. Remove all the flesh from one side before turning the fish over.

½ pint dry cider
½ pint liquid from cooking the salmon
½ teaspoon salt
1 bay leaf
12 black peppercorns
8 whole allspice
Pinch chilli powder
Finely pared rind ½ lemon
1 small onion
4 portions cooked salmon, off the bone

Combine the cider, cooking liquid, salt, bay leaf, peppercorns, allspice, chilli powder and lemon rind in a saucepan, bring to the boil and simmer for 15 minutes. Strain the marinade and leave to get cold. Peel the onion, cut into very thin slices and divide into rings. Arrange the salmon portions in a shallow dish, top with the onion rings, pour over the marinade and leave to chill in a refrigerator for at least four hours before serving. Serve with thin slices of cucumber and a mixed salad.

Anguilles Au Vert

The first time I went to Belgium I was taken to a marvellous restaurant in Brussels where I ate one of the best meals of my life and realized why it is that the Belgians are renowned for their food. Since then I buy eels whenever I find them in a fishmonger's – unfortunately, this doesn't happen nearly as often as I could wish.

2 lb eels
1½ ozs butter
1 tablespoon finely-chopped mint
2 teaspoons finely-chopped fresh sage (or ½ teaspoon dried sage)
2 tablespoons finely-chopped chervil or parsley
2 tablespoons finely-chopped sorrel (if possible)
½ pint dry white wine
⅓ pint water
2 egg yolks
Juice 2 lemons
Salt and freshly ground black pepper

Ask the fishmonger to remove the heads of the eels and to skin them for you. Cut the eels into 3-inch pieces. Melt half the butter in a heavy saucepan, add the herbs and eels, season with salt and pepper and simmer very gently for 15 minutes. Pour over the wine and water, bring to the boil and cook over a high heat for 10 minutes. Lift out the eels and arrange on a serving dish. Beat the egg yolks with the lemon juice until smooth and gradually add three tablespoons of the cooking liquid, stirring all the time. Add the remaining liquid, herbs and butter, check seasoning and pour the sauce over the eels.

Serve either hot or cold.

Mussels Concordia

Mussels are not always easy to get but when they are available they are inexpensive and, although they take time to prepare, their flavour justifies every second spent on their preparation. This is a tasty alternative to the more classical Moules Marinière and has the advantage of being able to be made in advance.

- 2 quarts mussels in the shell
- 1 oz butter
- 1 tablespoon flour
- 1 tablespoon finely-chopped parsley
- 2 tablespoons dry white wine
- 2 egg yolks
- 1 clove garlic
- 2 oz finely-grated cheese
- Pinch cayenne pepper

Scrub the mussels under cold water with a tough brush. Place them in a large saucepan without any additional liquid, cover the pan tightly and cook over a low heat for 6 minutes until all the mussels have opened. Strain the liquid through a fine sieve and leave the mussels to get cold. Remove the mussels from their shells and pull off the wiry beard from the centre. Melt the butter in a saucepan, add the very finely-chopped garlic and cook over a low heat for 2 minutes without browning. Add the flour and mix well. Gradually add ½ pint of the mussel liquid, stirring continually over a medium heat until the mixture is smooth and comes to the boil. Blend in the parsley and wine and season with salt and freshly ground black pepper. Beat the egg yolks until smooth. Add a little of the sauce and beat well. Add the egg yolk mixture to the sauce and beat over a low heat until the sauce is thick and shiny. Add the mussels, check the seasoning and turn into a shallow fireproof baking dish. Sprinkle with grated cheese, top with a little cayenne and put under a hot grill until the cheese has melted and is golden brown.

Moules Marinières

I rather feel that this aromatic concoction should be served as a main luncheon or supper dish rather than as a first course. It has a richness of flavour and of texture that makes it rather too substantial for a starter and in any case it deserves to be lingered over rather than just gulped down before something else.

2 quarts mussels
2 shallots (or 1 small onion)
1 clove garlic
1 bouquet garni
2 stalks celery
¼ pint white wine
⅛ pint water
2 egg yolks
2 tablespoons cream
2 tablespoons finely-chopped parsley
Freshly ground black pepper

Scrub the mussels under cold running water and discard any that are open. Finely chop the shallots and garlic and put them with the mussels into a large heavy saucepan. Add the mussels, bouquet garni and celery stalks, pour over the wine and water and season with plenty of freshly ground black pepper. Cover tightly and bring to the boil, shaking the pan every now and then to ensure an even distribution of heat. Lower the heat and simmer gently for 2–3 minutes until all the mussels are open. Remove the bouquet garni and celery stalks. Strain off the liquid into a clean pan.

Remove the beards (the wiry bit poking out) of the mussels, arrange them in four large bowls and keep warm. Beat the egg yolks with the cream and add to the mussel liquid. Heat through without boiling, stirring all the time until slightly thickened. Add the parsley, check seasoning and pour over the mussels.

Note: I recently learnt a nice little professional trick for eating mussels from the shell. Use an empty pair of shells as a natural instrument to pick out your mussels from their shells; the hinge is so strong it acts like a pair of pincers.

Leek Salad with Prawns

Leeks are even better cold than hot if you can find those small, thin and tender stalks at the beginning of the season. Served in this way they make a good lunch dish. The leeks should not be overcooked and should be very well drained – I do this by standing them upside down in a colander for at least 20 minutes.

12 slender leeks
2 hard-boiled eggs
1 tablespoon lemon juice
1 tablespoon milk
½ pint mayonnaise (see page 194)
Salt and pepper
½ lb peeled prawns

Clean the leeks well (dirt always seems to get between the leaves) and cook them in boiling salted water for about 15 minutes until just tender. Drain well and leave to cool.

Arrange the leeks in a shallow serving dish. Chop the egg whites and rub the yolks separately through a coarse sieve. Mix the lemon juice and milk with the mayonnaise and season with salt and pepper if necessary. Cover the leeks with the prawns mixed with the chopped egg white, pour over the mayonnaise and top with the egg yolks. Serve chilled.

Lobster Salad

Even a little lobster is better than nothing and a good way to stretch one small shellfish is to combine it in a luxury salad.

1 lobster
2 hard-boiled eggs
2 tomatoes
½ cucumber
1 lettuce
6 black olives
4 oz peeled prawns
¼ pint mayonnaise
1 tablespoon tomato ketchup
3 tablespoons sour cream

Split the lobster neatly down the back. Remove the stomach sack and the black line of intestine. Remove all the meat from the body and claws and reserve the head for garnishing. Chop the meat into 1-inch pieces. Shell and quarter the hard-boiled eggs. Peel and quarter the tomatoes. Peel the cucumber and cut the flesh into ½-inch thick lengths. Remove the outside of the lettuce and quarter the heart. Halve the olives and remove the stones. Arrange the lettuce heart around the outside of a glass bowl, with the hard-boiled eggs, tomatoes and cucumber. Place the lobster and prawns in the centre. Combine the mayonnaise, tomato ketchup and sour cream and mix well, pour the dressing over the shellfish and garnish with the black olives. Chill before serving.

Lemon Baked Fish

Use any good white fish for this dish. Cod will do but only if it is a middle cut and undoubtedly fresh. If possible, buy halibut, brill, or better still, turbot; the simplicity of this recipe deserves a first class base.

1 tablespoon olive oil
1 large onion
3 lemons
2 lb filleted white fish, with the skin removed
⅛ pint white wine
Salt and freshly ground black pepper
1 oz butter
½ teaspoon dill (finely-chopped if fresh)

Brush some of the olive oil over the bottom of a shallow baking dish. Peel and thinly slice the onion and divide into rings. Very thinly slice the lemons.

Arrange the onion slices on the bottom of the baking dish and cover with the fish fillets (cut into strips of 3–4 inches wide if cut from a large fish). Pour over the wine and remaining oil, season with salt and pepper and top with the thin slices of lemon arranged in an overlapping cover all over the fish. Bake in a moderately hot oven (400°F, Reg 6) for 20–25 minutes until the fish is just tender. Discard the lemons and the onion and reserve the cooking liquid. Arrange the fish on a heated serving dish and keep warm. Heat the butter over a low flame in a saucepan, add the chopped dill and the juices from the fish and season with a little salt and freshly ground black pepper. Pour the sauce over the fish just before serving.

Note: This dish can also be made with fillets of sole or plaice. In that case the fish will only need from 10–12 minutes cooking and will need to be skinned after cooking.

Plaice in Lemon and Prawn Sauce

1 small onion
½ pint white wine
1 pint water
1 bay leaf
Salt and pepper
4 large or 8 small plaice fillets
1½ oz butter
2 tablespoons flour
Juice ½ lemon
½ lb peeled prawns

Peel and slice onion and place it in a shallow frying pan with the white wine, water, bay leaf and seasoning. Bring to the boil and simmer for 5 minutes. Place fish fillets skin side up in the pan, cover and poach fish until skin will peel off – about 10 minutes. Lift out fish with a spatula and arrange in a lightly greased serving dish.

Strain fish stock into a clean pan and boil fast for 5 minutes. Measure ½ pint stock.

Melt butter in a saucepan, add flour and mix well. Gradually add fish stock, stirring continually over a medium heat until sauce is thick, smooth and shiny. Blend in lemon juice and check seasoning. Mix the prawns into the sauce and pour it over the fish. Heat through in a medium hot oven (375°F, Reg 5) for about 10 minutes.

Scallop and Bacon Kebabs

6 large scallops off the shell
Juice ½ lemon
Freshly ground black pepper
¼ lb small button mushrooms
1 green pepper
8 thin rashers bacon
2 tablespoons olive oil

Remove any black veins from the scallops and cut each one into four, making sure the red coral is intact in one quarter.

Sprinkle the scallops with lemon juice and pepper. Remove the stalks from the mushrooms. Remove the core and seeds of the green pepper, cut the flesh into ½-inch square pieces, blanch them in boiling water for five minutes and drain well. Remove the bacon rinds and stretch the rashers over the back of a knife. Cut each one in half and wrap each bit of bacon around a piece of scallop and thread them on four skewers, alternating with mushrooms and pieces of green pepper. Brush with olive oil and grill under a medium hot grill, turning frequently and basting the juices for 8–10 minutes.

Serve with Slim Jim Rice (see page 168) and a salad or green vegetable.

Scampi and Cucumber Salad

Scampi dipped in breadcrumbs and fried to a degree that results in them being crisp tit-bits of tastelessness have unfortunately become an all-too-common dish in the British Isles these days. When frozen scampi first appeared on the market there was a mad stampede to make use of them, but now they seem to have descended to the level of fish fingers. If you can get fresh scampi tails (and you can in some of the better fishmongers at certain times of the year) they are worth their weight in gold and in fact work out to be relatively inexpensive. Although fresh scampi are best for this delicious summer dish, the frozen varieties can successfully take their place.

1½ lb fresh scampi tails or 1 lb frozen scampi
½ cucumber
1 carton sour cream (5 fl oz)
¼ pint mayonnaise (see page 194)
2 teaspoons lemon juice
Salt and pepper
1 lettuce heart
1 green or red pepper for garnish

Peel freshly cooked scampi tails or steam de-frosted frozen

scampi in a colander for 5–8 minutes until just cooked, and leave to cool. Peel the cucumber and finely grate the flesh. Sprinkle it with salt and leave to sweat for an hour. Drain off excess liquid and pat cucumber dry on kitchen paper. Combine sour cream, mayonnaise and lemon juice. Mix well and season with salt and pepper. Blend in the cucumber and fold in the scampi. Finely shred the lettuce and cut the green or red pepper into thin rings, removing any seeds or core from the centre. Arrange the lettuce around the outside of a shallow serving dish, arrange the scampi salad in the centre and top with the pepper rings. Chill before serving.

(Quantities can be increased to serve as a main course).

Grilled Sole or Plaice with Orange Juice

The flavouring of citrus fruits goes well with most white fish. This is a simple dish but one that has great subtlety.

4 large or 8 small fillets of sole or plaice
1½ oz butter
Salt and freshly ground black pepper
Juice 1 large orange
Juice ½ lemon

Lay the fillets in a lightly greased fireproof dish and dot with small pieces of butter. Season the fish with salt and freshly ground black pepper. Combine the orange and lemon juice and pour half the liquid over the fish. Grill under a hot grill, as near to the flame as possible, for 4 minutes, pour over the remaining fruit juice and continue to grill for a further 4 minutes until the fish is cooked through and golden.

Serve with a green vegetable and a tomato salad.

Soles aux Fines Herbes

Plaice can be used instead of sole in this dish but the flavour is not so delicate.

- 1 small onion
- 4 water biscuits
- 2 oz butter
- 2 tablespoons finely-chopped parsley
- ¼ teaspoon tarragon
- 8 fillets of sole
- Salt and freshly ground black pepper
- ¼ pint dry white wine

Peel and finely chop the onion. Crush the water biscuits with a rolling pin until they resemble medium fine breadcrumbs. Use half the butter to grease a shallow fireproof dish. Spread the combined onion, 1 tablespoon parsley and the tarragon over the bottom of the dish and top with the fish fillets. Season with salt and freshly ground black pepper. Pour over the white wine and top with the biscuit crumbs. Dot with small pieces of the remaining butter. Bake the fish in a very moderate oven (350°F, Reg 4) for 20–30 minutes until the fish is tender. Brown under a hot grill for a minute or two and sprinkle with remaining parsley before serving.

Note: To make a more substantial dish, 4 oz of firm button mushrooms, finely chopped, can be added to the dish with the onion and parsley.

Hambledon Haddock

- 1 large onion
- 2 hard-boiled eggs
- 1 oz butter
- 2 cartons sour cream (10 fl oz)
- 1 tablespoon lemon juice
- 1 tablespoon white wine vinegar
- Salt and freshly ground black pepper
- Pinch paprika pepper
- 1½ lb fresh haddock fillets

Peel and finely chop the onion. Shell and chop the eggs. Heat the butter in a saucepan, add the onion and cook over a medium heat until the onion is soft. Add the sour cream, lemon juice and vinegar. Season with freshly ground black pepper and a little paprika and simmer gently for 10–15 minutes – do not boil. Fold in the hard-boiled eggs and check the seasoning.

Bring ¾ pint water to the boil in a shallow pan. Season with a little salt, add the fish and poach gently for about 15 minutes until tender. Drain well and remove the skin. Arrange the fish on a heated serving dish and pour over the sauce.

Smoked Haddock with Spinach

1½ lb smoked haddock
½ pint milk
½ pint water
1½ lb fresh spinach
1 tablespoon olive oil
1 small onion
2 firm ripe tomatoes
½ oz butter
4 tablespoons yoghurt
Salt and freshly ground black pepper

Poach the haddock in the combined milk and water for about 15 minutes until tender. Drain and remove any skin and bones and keep warm. Cook the spinach in boiling salted water for 5 minutes and drain well. Season with salt and pepper, add the olive oil and toss lightly. Arrange in a serving dish and keep warm.

Peel and very finely chop the onion. Peel the tomatoes (see page xii) and chop the flesh. Heat the butter, add the onion and cook over a moderate heat until the onion is soft. Add the tomatoes, season with salt and pepper and simmer for 5 minutes. Blend in the yoghurt and heat through without boiling. Arrange the fish on the spinach, spoon over the onions and tomatoes and serve at once.

Soused Herrings

Herrings are about the cheapest and most nutritious of foods. They have always made popular eating in this country and there are countless traditional recipes for serving them. This dish has a slightly sharp taste which counteracts the rather oily nature of the fish.

4 large or 8 small herrings
Salt and freshly ground black pepper
1 onion
1 dried chilli
1 bay leaf
¼ pint water
¼ pint white wine vinegar
4 whole allspice
Pinch mace
8 black peppercorns

Ask your fishmonger to scale and fillet the herrings. Season the fillets lightly with salt and freshly ground black pepper and roll each fillet up tightly, starting from the tail end. Peel and very thinly slice the onion and divide into rings. Chop the chilli. Arrange the rolled herrings in a fireproof baking dish, and arrange the onion rings and bay leaf on the top. Combine the water and white wine vinegar, add the spices and mix well. Pour the mixture over the fish (the fish and onions should be covered by the liquid) and cover with tinfoil. Bake in a very moderate oven (350°F, Reg 4) for 45 minutes. Leave the fish to cool in the liquid and serve cold with salad as a light luncheon or supper dish or on their own as a first course.

Grilled Herrings with Mustard Sauce

Herrings are one of the most valuable fish to swim in our seas. They contain a high level of protein and a generous amount of vital minerals. If they are fresh and shining when cooked, their taste can be exceptional.

4 herrings
1 oz softened butter
Juice ½ lemon
Salt and freshly ground black pepper
1 oz butter
1 tablespoon flour
1 carton sour cream (5 fl oz)
1 tablespoon French Dijon mustard

Clean and gut the herrings and cut three incisions diagonally across the sides of each fish. Rub the softened butter, lemon juice and seasoning into these incisions and grill the fish under a high heat for 3–4 minutes on each side. Keep warm whilst making the sauce.

Melt 1 oz butter in a saucepan, add the flour and mix well. Gradually blend in the sour cream over a low heat, stirring continually until the sauce is thick and smooth. Blend in the mustard and season with salt and pepper. Pour the sauce over the fish and serve at once.

Herrings with Sauce Analette

Grilled herrings with a sharp and rather unusual sauce. A good lunch or supper dish.

8 small herrings
Salt and pepper
A little olive oil
3 ripe tomatoes
1 small onion
1 tablespoon olive oil
1 teaspoon tomato purée
1 carton yoghurt
½ teaspoon tarragon
2 teaspoons French Dijon mustard

Clean herrings and remove heads and tails. Cut shallow slits, 1½ inches apart, on each side of the fish and rub skin with a little salt and pepper. Brush with a little olive oil and grill under a hot flame for about 5 minutes on each side until crisp and golden brown.

While fish are cooking, make the sauce: Peel and roughly

chop tomatoes. Peel and finely chop onion. Heat olive oil, add onions, tomatoes and tomato purée and cook over a low heat until onions are soft. Mix in yoghurt, tarragon and mustard. Season with salt and pepper and cook gently without boiling for a further 5 minutes. Pass the sauce through a fine sieve or a food mill, or blend in an electric liquidizer.

Pour the sauce over the herrings and serve at once.

Baked Mini Mackerel

Make this dish when mackerel are really small – the smaller they are the less oily and rich the fish will be and the flavour is delicious.

- 8 small mackerel
- ¼ lb green olives
- ¼ lb black olives
- 2 ripe tomatoes
- 1 tablespoon finely chopped parsley
- 1 tablespoon lemon juice
- 1 tablespoon French Dijon mustard
- 1 tablespoon olive oil
- Salt and freshly ground black pepper

Clean and gut the fish, leaving on the heads and tails, and arrange in a baking dish. Remove the stones of the olives and finely chop the flesh. Peel and chop the tomatoes and mix with the parsley and olives. Stuff the mackerel with the olives, tomatoes and parsley. Combine the lemon juice, mustard and oil, season with salt and pepper and mix well. Brush the mixture over the mackerel. Bake the fish in a moderate oven (375°F, Reg 5) for 20 minutes, basting every now and then with the juices in the pan.

Mackerel Fillets with Tomato and Horseradish Sauce

4 mackerel
1 pint water
2 tablespoons white wine vinegar
Salt and freshly ground black pepper
4 tomatoes
1 spring onion
1 carton sour cream (5 fl oz)
1 tablespoon grated horseradish
1 teaspoon lemon juice

Ask your fishmonger to fillet the mackerel. Poach the fillets in the water, with the vinegar and seasoning, for about ten minutes or until just tender. Drain well and leave to cool. Peel the tomatoes (see page xii) and remove the seeds and finely chop the flesh. Finely chop the spring onion. Combine the tomatoes, sour cream, onion, horseradish and lemon juice, season with salt and pepper, mix well and leave to stand for 10 minutes. Spread the sauce over the mackerel and chill well before serving.

Fillets of Mackerel with Sour Cream and Cucumber

4 mackerel
1 pint water
2 tablespoons white wine vinegar
Salt and freshly ground black pepper
1 cucumber
1 carton sour cream (5 fl oz)
1 tablespoon finely-chopped chives or parsley

Ask your fishmonger to fillet the mackerel. Poach the fillets in the water with the vinegar and seasoning for ten minutes or until just tender. Drain well and leave to cool. Remove the peel of the cucumber and coarsely grate the flesh. Sprinkle the cucumber with salt and leave to stand for 20 minutes. Drain off the excess liquid. Mix the cucumber with the sour cream, season with salt and pepper and spread the sauce over the mackerel fillets. Garnish with finely-chopped chives or parsley and chill before serving.

Cold Mackerel with Mustard Sauce

4 small mackerel
½ oz butter
1 tablespoon olive oil
Juice ½ lemon
2 egg yolks
⅛ pint olive oil
1 tablespoon French Dijon mustard
2 teaspoons white wine vinegar
½ teaspoon tarragon
Salt and freshly ground black pepper

Clean and gut the fish but leave the heads and tails on. Heat the butter and olive oil in a frying pan until foaming. Add the mackerel and cook over a high heat for 3–4 minutes on each side until crisp and golden. Drain really well on kitchen paper, leave to cool and sprinkle the fish with lemon juice. Beat the egg yolks until smooth and gradually add the olive oil, drop by drop, beating all the time until the mixture thickens and emulsifies. Blend in the mustard, vinegar and tarragon, season with salt and pepper and dribble the sauce over the cold mackerel. Chill before serving.

Paprika Fish

2 lb white fish fillets (turbot, haddock, cod, etc)
2 large onions
1½ tablespoons olive oil
⅓ pint water
1½ teaspoons paprika pepper
Salt

Skin the fish if necessary and cut into 2 inch wide strips. Peel the onions and divide into rings. Heat the olive oil in a large, heavy frying pan. Add the onions and cook over a medium heat until pale golden in colour. Blend in the water and paprika and season with salt. Add the pieces of fish, bring to the boil, cover and simmer for 20–30 minutes, depending on the thickness of the fish.

To serve, place the fish in the centre of a serving dish, surround with the onions and pour over the sauce.

Grilled Fillets of Fish Japanese Style

The Japanese have an unusual way of grilling fish with a glaze of egg yolks and rice wine which makes an exciting dish. This is an 'Anglified' version, using sherry rather than rice wine, but the finished effect is appetizing and attractive to look at. Any fillets of firm white fish can be used. The coating makes a golden finish and imparts a delicate taste to the fish as well as sealing in the natural juices.

8 small fillets white fish (sole, plaice, whiting, haddock, etc)
2 egg yolks
1 tablespoon sherry
Salt and freshly ground black pepper
Pinch cayenne pepper

Rub the fish fillets with salt and leave to stand for 15 minutes. Combine the egg yolks and sherry, and season with a little salt, freshly ground black pepper and a pinch of cayenne. Arrange the fillets on a fireproof dish and brush them with half the egg mixture. Grill under a medium hot heat for 5 minutes, turn over, brush with the remaining glaze and continue to grill for a further 5 minutes until cooked through and golden brown.

Grilled Fish with Lemon

Fresh white fish, rubbed with lemon juice, olive oil and seasoning are delicious. Choose small fish that will serve one person each and leave the heads and tails on. Use only better quality fish for this recipe such as red mullet, sea bass or, most delicious of all, John Dory when you can find them.

4 fish weighing about 8–12 oz each
1 large onion
4 sprigs parsley

2 tablespoons olive oil
Juice 1 lemon
Salt and freshly ground black pepper

Scale, gut and clean the fish (or ask your fishmonger to do
Peel the onion, cut into thin slices and divide into rings
the fish with the parsley sprigs, some onion rings and seasoning. Score the flesh of the fish with four shallow diagonal slashes on each side and brush them with the olive oil and lemon juice. Season with salt and pepper. Grill the fish under a hot flame for about 6 minutes on each side, basting frequently with the juices in the pan. Serve at once with lemon wedges.

A fresh tomato sauce goes well with this dish (see page 196).

Curried White Fish Salad

Cold curried fish might sound a bit strange but this combination makes an interesting and palatable dish for lunch in the summer – it can also be served in smaller quantities as a starter and can be garnished to look most attractive.

1½ lb white fish fillets (turbot, halibut or haddock)
1 clove garlic
2 onions
4 firm ripe tomatoes
1 green pepper

3 tablespoons olive oil
2 tablespoons tomato purée
½–1 teaspoon curry powder
1 tablespoon lemon juice
4 tablespoons home-made mayonnaise (see page 194)

Remove any skin and bones from the fish and cut the flesh into ½-inch pieces. Crush the garlic. Peel and thinly slice the onions and divide into rings. Peel the tomatoes (see page xii) and finely chop the flesh. Remove the core and seeds of the pepper and cut into very thin strips. Heat the olive oil, add the onions garlic and pepper and cook over a medium heat until the onions are soft. Add the tomatoes, tomato purée, curry powder, lemon juice, mix well and add the fish. Cook for 8–10 minutes until the fish is just tender and leave to cool.

Gently blend the mayonnaise into the fish and sauce, arrange in a serving dish and garnish with red pepper rings and slices of stoned black olives.

Braised Fish

This is a delicious way of cooking a whole fish such as a codling, sea bream, grey mullet (if you can get one) or haddock. The flavouring of the vegetables imparts a good taste to the fish and the flesh will be tender and moist.

2½ lb white fish
2 leeks
3 sticks celery
2 carrots
1 green pepper
3 tablespoons olive oil
1 small tin tomatoes
⅛ pint dry white wine
Salt and pepper
2 sprigs parsley or dill

Scale and clean the fish and remove the gills. Wash and thinly slice the leeks. Remove the leaves and thinly slice the celery. Peel and thinly slice the carrots. Remove the core and seeds of the green pepper and cut into thin slices. Heat 2 tablespoons olive oil in a heavy pan, add the leeks, celery, carrots and pepper and cook over a low heat for 15 minutes. Drain off the juice of the tomatoes and add the tomatoes to the other vegetables. Season with salt and pepper and arrange the vegetables in a shallow baking dish. Place the fish on the vegetables, rub the inside with the remaining olive oil, season with salt and pepper and stuff with the parsley or dill. Pour over the wine and tomato juice and bake in a moderate oven (375°F, Reg 5) for 30–45 minutes, basting with the juices every now and then.

Serve from the dish the fish was cooked in.

Marinated Kipper Salad

3 filleted kippers
4 hard-boiled eggs
2 tomatoes
1 green pepper
2 spring onions
6 tablespoons olive oil
2 tablespoons white wine vinegar
½ teaspoon French Dijon mustard
1 egg yolk
Salt and freshly ground black pepper
Pinch paprika pepper

Place the kippers in a shallow pan, cover with cold water and bring to the boil over a medium heat. Drain off the water and remove any small bones from the fish. Divide each fillet into 4 and place in a serving dish. Peel and chop the hard-boiled eggs. Skin the tomatoes (see page xii), remove the cores and roughly chop the flesh. Remove the core and seeds of the pepper and finely chop the flesh. Finely chop the spring onions. Add the eggs, tomatoes, pepper and onions to the kipper. Combine the olive oil, vinegar, mustard, egg yolk and seasoning in a screw-top jar and shake (or beat with a wire whisk) until the mixture is amalgamated. Pour the dressing over the salad ingredients, mix lightly and chill for at least an hour in a refrigerator before serving.

Serve with water biscuits or thinly-cut slices of buttered brown bread.

Light and enjoyable lunch and supper dishes which give pleasure without adding unwanted pounds or ounces

I think in these days of plenty, too many of us, have got into the habit of over-eating. It becomes a habit all too quickly and before you know where you are, the two main meals of the day become three-course feasts with one rich dish following another.

Two heavy meals during one day are not really in the least necessary and it's a good idea, if possible, to make sure that at least one meal a day is of a light variety. If you know you are dining out in the evening, then have a light lunch with one main dish and a salad followed by cheese or fruit. If you find yourself really tucking in in the middle of the day, then compensate by having a light supper. Light main course dishes are many and varied, covering a wide range from eggs to salads or fish – more substantial than a snack but low in calories and satisfying without being heavy.

Even though the main dish may be a light and simple one, there is no need to skimp on the garnishing or appearance of the dish. The look of food is always important and even a simple baked egg or hamburger can be made to look mouth-wateringly attractive if a little trouble is taken to serve it with flair. A few slices of tomato, a sprinkling of finely chopped parsley or some thinly sliced lemon won't add on any weight but it will add to your enjoyment of the food.

Hamburgers

'I'm slimming,' said my companion when we sat down to an expense-account lunch at a well-known restaurant, 'so I'll just have a little vichyssoise and a hamburger, very underdone.' She had the cheek to raise her eyebrows and give a scathing glance at my midriff when I ordered my favourite meal of a dozen oysters and a steak tartare.

The soup, correctly made with an almost equal quantity of potatoes and leeks and well topped-up with double cream, was followed by the largest hamburger I had seen for a long time, served on a mouthwateringly starchy brioche-type bun and was accompanied by a man-sized heap of French fries. She practically licked the plate with enjoyment and then smugly informed me that it was nice of me to ask her to lunch but, as I must realize, it was a bit of a waste as she never had more than the lightest snack in the middle of the day – because of her figure!

The anecdote might be funnier if this lady had, in fact, been large and swiftly heading for a heart attack, but I have to admit that she had the figure of a somewhat mature model and where she put all that food I will never know.

From the weightwatcher's point of view, there are hamburgers and hamburgers. If the cake is made from the leanest of minced meat, fried with the minimum of fat and served by itself with a salad, then it is indeed not a fattening dish but if it is produced as a traditional hamburger with all the trimmings you might just as well sit down to steak and kidney pie and mashed potatoes and have done with it.

Beware of shop-bought hamburgers or pre-minced meat as these are liable to contain a high quantity of fat and often breadcrumbs as well.

1½ lb rump steak
1 small onion
1 egg
Freshly ground black pepper
Few drops Worcestershire sauce
A little butter or oil
Salt

Trim off all the fat from the meat and pass it twice through a coarse mincer. Peel and finely chop or mince the onion. Combine the meat, onion and egg and mix well. Season with pepper and a few drops of Worcestershire sauce. Rub a frying pan with a little olive oil or butter to prevent the hamburgers sticking and heat it over a high flame. Add the hamburgers and cook over the highest possible heat for 1–2 minutes on each side. Season them lightly with salt and serve at once.

For a less expensive dish, use half minced rump steak and half very lean bacon.

Pig's Trotter Salad

If you have never bought a pig's trotter, now's the time to start. The meat is delicious, they are undeniably cheap, and can make an appetizing dish. This recipe for a salad can be served either as a first or main course.

8 unsalted pigs' trotters
4 sticks celery
6 large tomatoes
1 large onion
1 green or red pepper
¼ pint vinaigrette dressing (see page 191)
2 tablespoons finely-chopped parsley

Put the trotters into a saucepan, cover with cold water, bring to the boil and cook over a high heat for 1 hour. Lower the heat and simmer for a further 30 minutes. Plunge the trotters into cold water, remove the skin, cut the flesh off the bones and spread it on a plate to get cold (make sure the pieces of meat are separated or they will stick together).

Remove the leaves and thinly slice the celery stalks. Peel (see page xii) and chop the tomatoes. Peel and finely chop the onion. Remove the core and seeds of the pepper and chop the flesh. Combine the meat from the trotters the celery, onion, tomatoes and pepper in a serving bowl, pour over the dressing and toss lightly. Sprinkle over the parsley and chill well before serving.

Serves 8 as a first course or 4 as a main course

Devilled Kidneys

In the Victorian days, devilled kidneys were a breakfast or after dinner savoury dish. Today, most people would curl up their toes at the thought of eating such a strong dish for breakfast and they are more popular as a main course lunch or supper dish.

8 lambs' kidneys
2 teaspoons made English mustard
1 teaspoon lemon juice
Few drops Worcestershire sauce
Salt and cayenne pepper
2 onions
1 oz butter

Remove all the fat from the kidneys, remove the skins, cut each one in half and cut out the fatty cores. Combine the mustard, lemon juice, Worcestershire sauce and seasoning and spread the cut side of the kidneys with this mixture. Leave them to stand for at least one hour in a cool place. Peel and chop the onions. Melt the butter in a frying pan, add the onions and cook over a medium high heat until the onions are soft and golden. Remove the onions with a slotted spoon and keep warm. Raise the heat as high as possible, add the kidneys to the juices in the pan and cook them for 4 minutes, turning half-way through the cooking time. Return the onions to the pan and continue to cook for a further 2 minutes.

Serve with crisply fried bacon rashers, well drained on kitchen paper, and with a purée of runner beans (see page 157).

EGGS

Eggs, to me, are one of nature's marvels. What else is small, compact, perfectly packaged and full of protein? Their uses are thousandfold and their price still reasonable, considering their value.

Boiled, baked, scrambled and poached eggs make the basis of many delicious dishes; omelets provide one of the quickest and simplest of meals and can be made with an infinite variety of fillings. Egg yolks give sauces and soups a rich velvety texture and the whisked whites give a lightness to mousses and soufflés.

What is more, eggs are not fattening. The yolks, however, are high in cholesterol and eating too many eggs, I am told, is liable to make one aggressive. I eat them by the dozen and I don't think I have a tendency towards aggressiveness but these are perhaps two good reasons why one should avoid existing on a daily diet composed entirely of eggs.

Poached Eggs

Poached eggs, being cooked without any fat of any kind, are a boon for weight-watchers; the only trouble comes when you have to decide what to eat with them. Avoid thick slices of well-buttered toast to place under the egg or sauces thickened with lashings of cream.

Most experienced cooks have their own ways of cooking poached eggs. I myself abhor the method of steaming them in circular greased moulds – in sporting terms, I just don't think this 'cricket' and I was delighted to watch an American guest, breakfasting in a well known London hotel recently, who sent back his two poached eggs saying firmly that he wanted 'real poached eggs, not those uniform round things'. Almost as bad is the habit of putting a spoonful of vinegar into the water in which the eggs are to be cooked; I believe the idea is that this helps to prevent the whites of the eggs breaking but all it actually seems to do is make the finished eggs taste strongly of vinegar.

I poach mine in a fairly deep non-stick frying pan in about 1½–2 inches of water, cooking three eggs at a time. I drop the eggs into fairly fast boiling water and then cook them for about three minutes until just set. If the water gets messy, the pan must be rinsed out and fresh water put in before cooking the next batch. This seems to be satisfactory and fairly foolproof and, if the eggs are to be used cold, they can easily be trimmed to a neat shape with a pair of kitchen scissors or a circular pastry cutter.

Oeufs Florentine

6–8 poached eggs (see above)
12 oz frozen spinach (or 1 lb fresh spinach leaves)
Small knob of butter
½ tablespoon cream
Pinch nutmeg
1 oz butter
1 oz flour
½ pint milk
½ teaspoon French Dijon mustard
5 oz grated cheddar cheese

Cook the spinach until tender in boiling salted water and drain well in a colander, pressing to remove excess water. Mix in the knob of butter and cream and flavour with a small pinch of nutmeg. Arrange the spinach in a shallow fireproof baking dish. Place the poached eggs over the spinach.

Melt 1 oz butter in a saucepan, add the flour and mix well. Gradually blend in the milk over a medium heat, stirring continually until the sauce comes to the boil and is thick and smooth. Add the mustard and 4 oz of the cheese, season with salt and pepper, mix well and stir over a low heat until the cheese has melted. Pour the sauce over the eggs and top with remaining cheese. Brown in a hot oven or under a hot grill until the dish is hot through and the top is golden brown.

Portuguese Poached Eggs

¼ lb lean ham
6–8 poached eggs (see above)
2 onions
1 clove garlic
1 green pepper
2 tablespoons olive oil
1 small tin tomatoes (8 oz)
1 tablespoon tomato purée
Salt and pepper

Finely chop or mince the ham and spread it over the bottom of four individual fireproof dishes or one shallow fireproof baking dish. Arrange the poached eggs over the ham. Peel and thinly slice the onions. Peel and crush the garlic or press it through a garlic press. Remove the core and seeds of the pepper and cut the flesh into very thin rings. Heat the olive oil in a saucepan. Add the onion, garlic and pepper and cook over a medium heat for about 4 minutes until the onion is transparent. Add the tomatoes and tomato purée, mix well and season with salt and pepper. Bring to the boil, cover and simmer for 15 minutes.

Pour the sauce over the eggs and heat through in a very moderate oven (350°F, Reg 4) for 10–15 minutes until hot through.

Serve with Slim Jim Rice or one of the variations (see page 168).

Note: For a truly Mediterranean flavour, add a little oregano to the sauce.

Summer Eggs

The taste of eggs and lemon with tarragon is one that I find extremely pleasing, especially in the summer time. This dish makes a good hot weather lunch or supper main course when you are bored with cold meat and salads.

8 oz Slim Jim rice (see page 168)
6–8 poached eggs (see above)
1 oz butter
1 oz flour
⅛ pint milk
⅛ pint chicken stock
Juice ½ lemon
1 teaspoon tarragon
1 egg yolk
2 tablespoons cream
Salt and pepper

Spread the rice over the bottom of a shallow fireproof serving dish and top with the poached eggs. Heat the butter in a saucepan, add the flour and mix well. Gradually blend in the milk and chicken stock, stirring continually until the mixture comes to the boil and is thick and smooth. Add the lemon juice and tarragon, season with salt and pepper and simmer for four minutes. Beat the egg yolk into the cream and add to the sauce, heating through without boiling. Pour the sauce over the eggs and heat in a very moderate oven (350°F, Reg 4) for 10–15 minutes until hot through.

Serve with a green vegetable or salad.

Eggs Alexandra

A light but well-flavoured dish which makes a non-fattening but satisfying meal.

1 lb leaf spinach
2 teaspoons lemon juice
1½ tablespoons olive oil
Pinch nutmeg
6 eggs
1 small onion
1 clove garlic
1 small tin tomatoes
½ tablespoon tomato purée
Pinch oregano
2 oz finely-grated cheddar or Gruyère cheese
Salt and freshly ground black pepper

Wash the spinach and discard any tough stalks. Place the spinach in a saucepan without any extra water. Season with a little salt, cover and simmer for 10 minutes until the spinach is just tender. Mix in the lemon juice and ½ tablespoon olive oil, season with salt, pepper and a pinch nutmeg and arrange in a fireproof baking dish. Poach the eggs until lightly set, drain them well and place them on top of the spinach.

Peel and finely chop the onion and crush the garlic. Heat 1 tablespoon olive oil in a saucepan, add the onion and garlic and cook over a moderate heat until the onion is soft and transparent. Mix in the tomatoes, tomato purée and oregano and season with salt and freshly ground black pepper. Cover and simmer for 10 minutes. Pour the tomato sauce over the eggs, top with grated cheese and brown under a hot grill until the cheese has melted and the dish is hot through.

BAKED EGGS OR OEUFS EN COCOTTE

These simple little dishes have an infinite number of varieties, few of which can in any way be called fattening (unless, of course, they are made with lashings of butter and cream, neither of which are in any way necessary to the enjoyment of the final article).

Serve the eggs as a light first course or as a simple main dish for lunch or supper, followed by a salad. For a main dish, allow 2 eggs per serving.

Plain Baked Eggs

½ oz butter
4 eggs
2 tablespoons milk
Salt and freshly ground black pepper

Lightly butter four ramekin dishes. Break an egg into each dish, top with a little milk and season with a little salt and freshly ground black pepper. Place the eggs in a baking dish half full of hot water and bake in a very moderate oven (350°F, Reg 4) for 10 minutes or until the eggs are just set.

Baked Eggs with Mushrooms and Tomato

2 oz mushrooms
½ oz butter
1 tablespoon tomato ketchup
4 eggs
2 tablespoons top of milk
Salt and freshly ground black pepper

Finely chop the mushrooms. Heat the butter in a saucepan, add the mushrooms and cook over a high heat, stirring continually for 3 minutes. Mix in the tomato ketchup and season with salt and pepper. Divide the mushroom mixture between four ramekin dishes, break over the eggs, top with milk and cook in the same way as 'Plain Baked Eggs'.

Baked Egg with Smoked Salmon

Smoked salmon and eggs make a beautiful combination; in this recipe a little smoked salmon goes a long way and makes a really first-class starter to a meal.

½ oz butter
2 oz smoked salmon
4 eggs
2 tablespoon sour cream
Salt and a pinch of cayenne pepper

Very finely chop the smoked salmon and divide it between the bottom of 4 buttered ramekin dishes. Break over the eggs and top with the sour cream. Season with a tiny amount of salt and a small pinch of cayenne and cook in the same way as 'Plain Baked Eggs'.

Portuguese Baked Eggs

1 small onion
1 large ripe tomato
½ tablespoon olive oil
1 tablespoon chopped green pepper
4 eggs
Salt and freshly ground black pepper

Peel and finely chop the onion. Peel the tomato (see page xii), discard the seeds and finely chop the flesh. Heat the olive oil in a small saucepan, add the onion and the deseeded, chopped green pepper and cook over a medium heat for 5 minutes until the onion and pepper are soft. Add the tomato, season with salt and pepper and simmer for 5 minutes. Divide the onion mixture between 4 ramekin dishes, break over the eggs and cook in the same way as 'Plain Baked Eggs.'

Baked Eggs with Prawns

½ oz butter
4 oz peeled prawns
2 tablespoons sour cream
1 tablespoon sherry
Few drops Tabasco sauce
4 eggs
1 oz finely-grated cheddar cheese
Pinch paprika pepper

Melt the butter, add the prawns, sour cream and sherry and flavour with a few drops of Tabasco. Heat, without boiling, over a low flame for 3 minutes and divide between 4 ramekin dishes. Break over the eggs, top with grated cheese and a light dusting of paprika and cook as for 'Plain Baked Eggs'.

Omelet Supreme

An omelet may be one of the quickest and most simple of dishes to produce but it can also be one of the most dramatic. This is one such dish: a light, succulent egg mixture filled with a luscious combination of red caviar (salmon roe), sour cream and spring onions.

6 eggs
1 tablespoon water
Salt and pepper
1 oz butter
1 jar red caviar
1 carton sour cream (5 fl oz)
4 spring onions

Beat the eggs with a fork until yolks and whites are well broken, blend in the water and season lightly with salt and pepper. Heat a quarter of the butter in a small omelet pan, add a quarter of the egg mixture and cook over a medium high heat until the omelet is light brown on the bottom and only just cooked on the top. Spread a spoonful of the caviar and the sour cream across the centre, season very lightly and place a spring onion across the top of the filling. Slide the omelet on to a heated serving dish, folding it in half as you do so. Keep warm whilst cooking the remaining omelets in the same way.

Serve as soon as the omelets are all cooked.

Omelet Alfonse

6 eggs
4 tablespoons sour cream
2 oz ham
2 oz cooked carrots
2 oz cooked peas
Salt and pepper
1 oz butter
2 oz grated cheese

Beat eggs with a fork or wire whisk. Add 2 tablespoons sour cream and mix well. Finely chop ham and carrots and add to the egg mixture with the peas. Season with salt and pepper and mix well. Heat the butter in an omelet pan. Add omelet mixture and cook over a medium heat, scoring through the omelet with a knife to ensure even cooking, for about six minutes or until the eggs are *just* set. Transfer the omelet on to a heated serving dish, folding it in half. Mix remaining cream with the cheese and spread over the omelet. Brown quickly under a hot grill. Serve at once with a green or mixed salad.

Chinese Omelet

4 oz cooked chicken
1 small onion
1 celery stalk
1 small tin bean sprouts
3 tablespoons olive oil
1 tablespoon deseeded, finely-chopped green pepper
6 eggs
Salt and pepper

Finely chop the chicken. Peel and finely chop the onion. Finely chop the celery and drain off the liquid from the bean sprouts. Heat 1 tablespoon olive oil in a frying pan, add the bean sprouts, onion, celery and green pepper and cook over a low heat for about ten minutes until the celery and pepper are tender. Drain off any excess liquid. Lightly beat the eggs, add the chicken and vegetables and season with salt and pepper. Heat the remaining olive oil in an omelet pan, add a thin layer of the omelet mixture and cook over a medium high heat, turning once until golden brown on each side. Remove on to a heated serving dish and keep warm while the remaining omelets are cooked.

Sprinkle with a few drops of soy sauce before serving.

Omelet Arnold Bennett

In this recipe I have substituted sour cream for the more usual double cream in the classic dish. If anything, I think the taste is improved as the double cream tends to make it a little too rich.

1 lb smoked haddock
½ pint milk
½ pint water
1 carton sour cream (5 fl oz)
4 eggs, separated
2 oz grated Parmesan cheese
Salt and freshly ground black pepper

Poach the haddock for 15 minutes in the combined milk and

water. Leave to cool and remove any skin and bones. Combine the haddock with half the sour cream and season with freshly ground black pepper.

Beat the egg yolks and season with a little salt. Fold in half the cheese and the fish/cream mixture. Beat the egg whites until stiff and lightly fold them into the other ingredients. Heat the butter in an omelet pan, add the omelet mixture and cook over a medium high heat, scoring through with a knife from time to time to ensure even cooking, until the omelet is firm and golden on the underside but still liquid on the top. Slide the omelet on to a fireproof dish, fold in half and spread with the remaining cream mixed with the remaining cheese. Brown quickly under a very hot grill and serve at once.

Leek and Ham Omelet

A rather unusual omelet which makes a good lunch or supper dish. In France it is sometimes served as a starter but I feel that makes rather too rich a meal.

1 lb leeks (preferably young, slim ones)
¼ lb ham
6 eggs
½ tablespoon olive oil
Salt and pepper

Trim off the coarse green tops of the leeks, wash and drain them well and cook them in boiling salted water for about 15 minutes until just tender. Place the leeks upside down in a colander and leave to drain and cool. Cut the cooled leeks into ½ inch slices. Chop the ham and beat the eggs lightly with a wire whisk. Add the leeks and ham to the eggs, season with salt and pepper and mix lightly.

Heat the oil in an omelet pan until smoking. Pour in the egg mixture and cook over a medium high heat, scoring the omelet through with a knife to allow the runny egg to slip through to the bottom as the omelet cooks. When the omelet is *just* set, slide it on to a heated serving dish and serve at once, cut into wedges like a cake.

Serve with a salad or green vegetable.

Eggs Christine

Christine, my son's nanny and a beautiful redhead, has been an inspiration in my life. A dedicated vegetarian, she leads me into experimenting with a wide range of meatless main courses which I might otherwise never come across. As a result, my housekeeping bills have (amazing in this day and age) actually gone down and we have at least one meatless meal a day.

6 eggs
1½ oz butter
½ lb mushrooms
½ teaspoon lemon juice
1 tablespoon flour
½ pint milk
3 oz finely-grated cheddar cheese
1 teaspoon French Dijon mustard
Salt and pepper
Pinch paprika pepper
2 eggs

Cook six eggs in boiling water for exactly five minutes. Cool them at once under cold water and carefully remove the shells. Very thinly slice the mushrooms. Melt ½ oz of the butter in a non-stick frying pan, add the mushrooms and cook over a high heat for 3 minutes, shaking the pan to prevent them burning (they should be golden brown but not blackened). Flavour the mushrooms with a little lemon juice and season with salt and pepper. Arrange the mushrooms in the bottom of a souffle dish and top with the boiled eggs.

Melt the remaining butter in a saucepan, add the flour and mix well. Gradually add the milk, stirring continually over a medium heat until the sauce is thick and smooth. Mix in 2 oz grated cheese and the mustard, season with salt, pepper and a pinch of paprika and cook over a low heat for 2 minutes until the cheese has melted. Separate two eggs and beat the yolks into the sauce. Whip the egg whites until stiff and fold them lightly into the sauce. Pour the sauce over the eggs, top with remaining grated cheese and bake in a very moderate oven (350°F, Reg 4) for 30 minutes until well risen and golden brown. Serve at once with a green or mixed salad, or a green vegetable.

Portuguese Scrambled Eggs

Good, richly yellow scrambled eggs with a shining, rather liquid texture go well with anything. In Portugal they are often served with a mixture of vegetables and make a satisfying dish.

6 eggs
2 tablespoons top of milk
1 onion
2 courgettes (zucchini)
1 lb tomatoes
2 green or red peppers
1 tablespoon olive oil
1 oz butter
Salt and pepper

Beat the eggs lightly with the milk and season with salt and pepper. Peel and finely chop the onion. Cut the courgettes into small dice. Peel the tomatoes (see page xii), remove the seeds and cut the flesh into small pieces. Remove the core and the seeds of the peppers, cut the flesh into small pieces and blanch them in boiling water for three minutes – drain well. Heat the olive oil in a saucepan, add the onion and cook over a low heat for about three minutes until the onion becomes soft and transparent. Add the courgettes, tomatoes and peppers, season with salt and pepper and cook over a low heat, stirring from time to time, for about 20 minutes until the vegetables are soft.

Melt half the butter in a non-stick saucepan. Add the eggs and cook over a low heat, stirring occasionally, for 4 minutes. Mix in the rest of the butter cut into small pieces and continue to cook until the eggs are just setting. Arrange the scrambled eggs in the centre of a heated serving dish and surround with the vegetables.

Curried Eggs

Serve these hot as a light main course or cold as a substantial starter. The taste of curry is not over-strong but the end result has the subtle flavouring of an Eastern dish.

6 hard-boiled eggs
2 onions
1 cooking apple
½ oz butter
1 tablespoon olive oil
1 tablespoon curry powder
2 teaspoons tomato purée
½ pint hot chicken stock (or water and stock cube)
1 teaspoon lemon juice
1 tablespoon sultanas
1 tablespoon finely-chopped parsley

Shell and halve the hard-boiled eggs. Peel and thinly slice the onions and divide into rings. Peel the apples, core and cut into small dice. Melt the butter and oil in a frying pan, add the onions and cook over a medium low heat until the onions are soft and transparent. Blend in the curry powder and tomato purée and mix well. Add the stock and cook over a medium heat, stirring continually for 5 minutes. Add the lemon juice, apple and sultanas and continue to cook for a further 8 minutes until the apple is soft. Add the eggs, heat through and transfer to a serving dish.

Serve hot or cold with a garnish of finely-chopped parsley.

Egg and Consommé Mousse

6 hard-boiled eggs
1 tin consommé
1 tablespoon tomato purée
1 teaspoon lemon juice
¼ teaspoon sage
2 tablespoons sour cream
½ teaspoon Worcestershire sauce
1 tomato

Peel and chop the hard-boiled eggs. Heat the consommé until melted, blend in the tomato purée, lemon juice and sage and simmer over a low heat for five minutes. Strain through a fine sieve and leave to cool.

Combine the chopped eggs, sour cream, Worcestershire sauce and half the consommé and turn into a serving dish or glass bowl. Set until firm in a refrigerator, pour over the remaining consommé mixture and return to the refrigerator until the surface is firm. Garnish with slices of peeled tomato and serve well chilled.

Chopped Chicken Liver and Hard Boiled Eggs

This is a traditional Jewish hors d'oeuvre, but as it makes a rather rich dish I prefer to serve it as a main course for lunch or supper. Be careful not to overcook the livers as this makes them tough and ruins the flavour; they should be nicely pink on the inside. Serve it as a main course with a salad and Melba toast. The mixture is smooth and rather like a pâté in texture.

¾ lb chicken livers
1 large onion
2 tablespoons chicken dripping or olive oil
2 hard-boiled eggs
1 small clove garlic (optional)
Salt and freshly ground black pepper

Remove any tough fibres from the livers. Peel and roughly

chop the onion. Heat the dripping or olive oil, add the onion and cook over a medium heat until transparent – about 3 minutes. Raise the heat, add the livers and brown quickly on all sides and drain off the juice. Shell the eggs and separate the whites from the yolks. Mince the onions, chicken livers and egg whites through the fine blades of a mincing machine (the mixture should be smooth and creamy and may have to be minced twice). Blend in the juices from the pan and season with salt and freshly ground black pepper. Add the garlic, squeezed through a garlic press, if the taste of garlic is liked. Spread the mixture in a shallow serving dish.

Rub the egg yolks through a coarse sieve and sprinkle them over the liver pâté. Chill before serving.

Stilton Soufflé

A good luncheon dish to serve as a main course with a salad.

5 oz Stilton cheese
2 oz butter
2 oz flour
1 pint milk
1 teaspoon made English or Dijon mustard
4 eggs, separated
Salt and pepper

Mash Stilton with a fork. Melt butter, add flour and mix well. Gradually add milk, stirring continually until the mixture comes to the boil and is thick and smooth. Add Stilton and mustard. Mix well and remove from the heat. Add egg yolks one by one, beating well after each addition. Season with salt and pepper. Beat egg whites until stiff and fold lightly into soufflé base. Turn into a lightly greased soufflé dish and bake in a moderately hot oven (400°F, Reg 6) for 40 minutes.

Cottage Cheese Salad

The sort of dish to have for lunch the day after you have over-indulged at someone else's dinner party.

2 celery stalks
2 spring onions
½ lb cottage cheese
1 tablespoon chopped red or green pepper
½ teaspoon Worcestershire sauce
2 drops Tabasco sauce
1 bunch watercress
Paprika pepper
Salt and freshly ground black pepper

Finely chop the celery. Very thinly slice the spring onions. Combine the cottage cheese with the pepper, celery and spring onions and mix in the Worcestershire sauce and Tabasco. Season with salt and pepper and arrange the salad on a bed of watercress leaves dipped into French dressing. Sprinkle the cheese with a little paprika and chill before serving.

Serves 2

Main courses compiled with the tape measure in mind

Minced Meat in Cabbage Leaves

If you buy your meat ready minced from the butcher, make sure that it is fresh and really lean. A pound of minced meat can make a good and inexpensive dish for four.

1 clove garlic
1 onion
1 lb lean minced meat
2 tablespoons very finely-chopped parsley
8 large white cabbage leaves
½ pint stock
1 tablespoon tomato purée
Salt and freshly ground black pepper

Press the garlic through a garlic press. Peel and finely chop the onion. Combine the meat, garlic, onion and parsley, season with salt and freshly ground black pepper and mix well. Drop the cabbage leaves into a large saucepan of boiling, salted water and cook for 5 minutes. Drain the leaves and pare down the stalks to the same thickness as the leaf part. Divide the meat filling between the leaves, fold in the sides and roll up neatly. Place the rolls in a lightly-greased baking dish. Bring the stock to the boil and blend in the tomato purée. Pour the stock over the cabbage leaves (the liquid should just cover the rolls) and bake in a very moderate oven (350°F, Reg 4) for 1 hour.

Braised Beefsteak

A classic French dish which takes some time to cook but which results in the meat being mouthwateringly tender and superbly flavoured. Unlike most ways of cooking steak, this dish can be cooked in advance and, in fact, benefits from being reheated.

2 lb rump steak
¼ lb thickly-cut bacon rashers
8 peppercorns
2 onions
1 large carrot
1 tablespoon flour
½ pint good stock
Bouquet garni
4 bay leaves
2 tablespoons brandy
Salt
1 tablespoon finely-chopped parsley

Remove the fat from the meat and cut into 8 even pieces. Remove the rinds and roughly chop the bacon. Coarsely crush the peppercorns. Peel and chop the onions. Peel and cut the carrot into small dice.

Fry the bacon, without extra fat, in a heavy flameproof casserole, over a medium low heat until all the fat has been melted. Raise the heat, add the steaks and brown quickly on all sides. Remove the bacon and meat, add the flour to the juices in the pan and mix well. Blend in the stock, stirring continually over a medium heat until the sauce is thick and smooth. Add the onions, carrots, peppercorns, bouquet garni, bay leaves, brandy, meat and bacon and season with salt. Simmer gently for 2–2½ hours until the meat is really tender. Remove the bouquet garni and bay leaves, check the seasoning and sprinkle with parsley before serving.

Note: The dish can be cooked in a very moderate oven (325°F, Reg 3) for about the same length of time.

Eastern Meat Casserole

A spicy dish flavoured with garlic, turmeric and chilli.

1½ lb lean stewing beef
2 cloves garlic
4 stalks celery
2 green or red peppers
3 tablespoons olive oil
1 teaspoon chilli powder
¼ teaspoon turmeric
¾ pint water or light stock
Juice 1 lemon
1 carton yoghurt (5 fl oz)

Trim off all the fat from the beef and cut the meat into neat 1-inch cubes. Peel and crush the garlic. Thinly slice the celery. Remove the core and seeds from the peppers and cut the flesh into thin strips. Heat the oil in a heavy fireproof casserole. Add the garlic and cook over a moderate heat for about 2 minutes until the garlic is soft and transparent. Raise the heat, add the meat and cook over a high heat until the meat is well-browned on all sides. Add the celery, red pepper, chilli and turmeric and mix well. Blend in the water or stock and the lemon juice, cover tightly and simmer gently for 1 hour.

Remove from the heat and blend in the yoghurt. Serve with rice or a purée of green beans and a green vegetable or salad.

Basonover Beef

A quickly-made dish with a rich exciting colour; avoid using tinned beetroot which usually have sugar added to their juice.

2 onions
½ lb cooked beetroot
1 tablespoon capers
2 tablespoons olive oil
1½ lb good minced beef
1 teaspoon sherry sauce* or a few drops Tabasco
2 tablespoons finely-chopped parsley
1 carton sour cream (5 fl oz)
Salt and freshly ground black pepper

Peel and finely chop the onion. Cut the beetroot into small dice. Finely chop the capers. Heat the olive oil in a large frying pan, add the onions and cook over a low heat for five minutes until they are transparent. Turn up the heat, add the beef and brown quickly. Mix in the beetroot, sherry sauce, capers and parsley and cook over a low heat for about ten

*A bottled sauce available from good delicatessen shops.

minutes until the beef is tender. Mix in the sour cream and season with salt and pepper.

Serve with a salad or a green vegetable.

Serves 6

STEAK

Steak is the slimmer's classic main course – full of protein, low in calories and great if you can afford it, and if you can, here are a few pointers towards producing the real McCoy.

If you are going to settle for a horrifically expensive cut of meat such as a top quality steak, then treat it with respect and don't detract from its superb taste by disguising the flavour with heavy or rich sauces. In the same way, if you have decided to go bust on good steak then make sure you really are getting the best, don't cut corners by buying from a cheap, second-rate butcher or by buying cheaper deep frozen products . . . you would be better off in the long run by settling for stewing steak and making it into a first-rate casserole or stew.

Good steak should be cut from a well-hung animal, be a rich, bloody red in colour and, if it has fat, the fat should be a rich yellow; these days even good butchers have problems with hanging so it is advisable to wrap the meat with a light covering of greaseproof paper and to keep it in your refrigerator to mature the flavour for about three days before cooking it.

Good steaks are better and need less cooking fats or oils if you grill rather than fry them; the quick cooking seals in the juices and the direct heat gives a truly browned surface.

In France they tend to spoil the meat with a well-laced accompanying sauce and it was in Italy that I discovered the secret of steak perfection when I ate in small cafés in the Venice area and tasted a series of blissful pieces of meat which had been brushed with good quality olive oil, seasoned with freshly ground black pepper and which were served with generous quarters of lemon. The absence of salt in the cooking meant that all the juices remained in the meat instead of being drawn out by the salt and the addition of lemon juice enhanced all the true flavours.

The basic English cuts of steak for grilling:
Fillet: The most expensive cut with fat and gristle trimmed off – very tender. Thick slices are called tournedos and smaller ones mignons.
Rump: Not as tender as fillet but with more taste – cut in ½-inch slices.
Entrecote: Cut from the top of the sirloin and on a par with rump.

Grilled Steak with Lemon

4 steaks (allow from 6–8 ozs per portion)
Olive oil
Freshly ground black pepper
1 large lemon

Trim off any fat from the steaks and brush on both sides with olive oil. Season both sides of the meat with freshly ground black pepper.

Heat the grill for at least 5 minutes before beginning to cook the steaks; both the flame and the grill rack should have time to get really red hot. Grill the steaks for one minute on each side to brown and seal the meat, lower the heat just a little and continue cooking the meat for a further three to eight minutes, turning every now and then, depending on the thickness of the meat and the desired rareness – personally I like my steak a rich brown on the outside and really red in the centre, but that depends entirely on taste. Sprinkle the cooked steaks with a little salt, arrange on a heated serving dish, garnish each one with a quarter of lemon and serve *at once* – if a steak is kept warm it will inevitably go on cooking.

Serve the steak with a green or mixed salad.

It isn't always possible to cook steak for guests at the last minute; one way round this is to have a good table cooker, one of the pressurized butane gas varieties, and to cook the main course at the table – the effect isn't the same because the heat isn't as strong but it is a popular way of producing an instant main course.

Fried Steak with Lemon

- 4 steaks (see above) – allow 6–8 oz per serving
- ½ oz butter
- 1 tablespoon olive oil
- Freshly ground black pepper
- Salt
- 1 large lemon

Trim off any fat and gristle from the steaks and season them on both sides with a little freshly ground black pepper. Heat a little of the butter and olive oil in a heavy-bottomed frying pan until smoking, add the steaks and fry very quickly for 1 minute on each side to brown thoroughly. Lower the heat a little and continue to cook, turning if necessary, for another 3–8 minutes, depending on the thickness of the meat. Sprinkle with salt and serve at once with quarters of lemon and the juices from the pan poured over the meat.

Accompany with a green or mixed salad.

Despite everything I have said about the perfect steak, some people really do prefer it with a little added flavouring. One of the most popular recipes under this heading is Steak au Poivre (a fillet steak cooked with a coating of crushed peppercorns). This used to be made with common or garden black peppercorns but now fresh 'green' peppercorns can be bought from good delicatessens in tins and these have a far less harsh and more subtle flavouring. Drain off the liquid from the green peppercorns before using them.

Steak au Poivre

- 4 fillet steaks
- 2 tablespoons black (or tinned green) peppercorns
- 1 oz butter
- 1 tablespoon olive oil
- Salt
- 2 tablespoons brandy

Trim off any fat and gristle from the steaks. Crush the peppercorns with a pestle and mortar or with a rolling pin until they resemble coarse breadcrumbs. Press the peppercorns into both sides of the steaks.

Heat enough of an equal quantity of the butter and olive oil to form a thin film across the bottom of a thick-bottomed frying pan. When the fat is really hot and smoking, add the steaks and cook for 1 minute, turning once. Lower the heat and continue cooking for a further 3–5 minutes depending on the thickness of the steaks. Arrange the steaks on a heated serving dish, add the remaining butter and oil to the pan and when the butter has melted add the brandy, bring to the boil and cook for a minute, pour the juices over the steak and serve at once.

Accompany with a green or mixed salad.

Steak can be disappointing – if you have qualms don't take risks but add flavour and tenderness by beating and marinading the meat. Here is a trustworthy recipe for steak which may not be as tender as it ought to be.

- 1 onion
- 1 clove garlic
- 2 tablespoons olive oil
- 2 tablespoons red wine vinegar
- Pinch thyme
- 2 bay leaves
- Salt and freshly ground black pepper
- 1 teaspoon French Dijon mustard
- 4 steaks (6–8 oz each)

Peel, thinly slice the onion and divide into rings. Peel and crush the clove of garlic. Mix the oil and vinegar, add the thyme and bay leaves and season with salt and pepper and mustard. Add the onion and garlic. Put the steak into a narrow bowl and pour over the marinade. Leave to stand in a cold place for 24 hours, drain off the marinade and lightly pat the meat with kitchen paper. Heat a heavy frying pan without any fat. Add the steaks and cook over a high heat for one minute on each side, lower the heat and continue to cook for 3–5 minutes depending on the thickness. Place the steaks on a heated serving dish, garnish with parsley, pour over the juices from the pan and serve with grilled tomatoes and a green salad.

Steak Selina

If you are planning a dinner party, steak cooked in the normal way can be a problem – it has to be cooked at the last minute and you may not want to leave your guests to their own devices while you go off by yourself to stand over a hot stove. Steak Selina is a method of cooking steak which can be done in advance and although the meat doesn't have that marvellous pink texture inside it does make a very acceptable main course.

2 lb fillet in one piece
2 onions
1 oz butter
½ tablespoon olive oil
2 tablespoons brandy
1 tin consommé
1 tablespoon tomato purée
3 tablespoons sour cream
1 tablespoon finely-chopped parsley
Salt and freshly ground black pepper

Trim off any fat or gristle from the meat and cut the fillet into 8 thin slices. Peel and very thinly slice the onions and divide them into rings. Heat the butter and oil in a frying pan, add the onion rings and cook over a medium low heat until the onions are soft and transparent. Remove the onions with a slotted spoon and arrange them in the bottom of a heavy casserole dish. Add the meat to the juices in the frying pan and brown quickly on both sides over a high heat. Heat the brandy in a small saucepan, pour it over the meat and light it with a match. Shake the pan until the flames die down, arrange the meat over the onions and season with salt and pepper. Mix the consommé and tomato purée together and pour them over the meat. Cook in a moderate oven (375°F, Reg 5) for 30 minutes until the meat is tender.

Transfer the meat and onions to a serving dish and add the sour cream and parsley to the sauce. Heat through, check seasoning and pour the sauce over the meat.

Braised Brisket of Beef

Brisket is a useful joint, lean and not too expensive. Cooked in the oven, wrapped in a tinfoil parcel, it makes a tender and delicious main course.

2 tablespoons olive oil or meat dripping
3 lb rolled brisket
1 onion
2 tomatoes
1 tablespoon tomato purée
2 tablespoons white wine
Salt and freshly ground black pepper

Heat the olive oil or dripping in a large heavy frying pan. Add the meat and brown quickly on all sides. Peel and roughly chop the onion. Chop the tomatoes. Place the meat and onion on a large piece of tinfoil. Top with the tomatoes mixed with the tomato purée. Season with salt and freshly ground black pepper, seal into a neatly-wrapped parcel and place in a baking tin. Cook the meat in a hot oven (450°F, Reg 8) for 2 hours. Unwrap the meat and keep it warm. Strain off the juices and combine them in a saucepan with the white wine. Heat through, adjust the seasoning if necessary, and remove any fat from the surface.

Serve the meat with stuffed onions and a green vegetable.

Serves 6

Boeuf Stroganoff

Considering this is one of the world's classic dishes, it is amazing how often people ruin it. The dish must be made with the best fillet steak and the secret lies in a minimum of cooking and serving as soon as possible; in this way the full flavour of the meat is retained and it should be as soft as butter; overcooking toughens the meat.

1½ lb fillet steak
2 onions
1 tablespoon olive oil
1 oz butter
¼ pint good red wine
Salt and pepper
1 carton sour cream (5 fl oz)

Remove any fat or gristle from the meat and cut it into thin strips about ½-inch wide and 2 inches long. Peel and chop the onions. Heat the olive oil and butter in a heavy frying pan. Add the onions and cook over a medium heat until they are soft and transparent. Remove the onions with a slotted spoon, raise the heat as high as possible, wait until the pan is red hot and add the meat, browning it quickly on all sides. Lower the heat as soon as the meat is browned, add the softened onions and pour over the red wine. Season with salt and pepper and cook for no longer than three minutes. Mix in the sour cream, heat through and serve at once.

English Boiled Beef

It doesn't sound exciting but I can promise you that a really good piece of beef, boiled with plenty of vegetables is one of the most delicious dishes ever thought of. Serve the joint with a sour cream horseradish sauce made from some of the stock and use the remaining stock (well skimmed of all the fat) for soups or sauces. If there is any beef over, use that to make the base of some of the meat salads in the salad section.

3 carrots
2 stalks celery with the leaves
2 onions
1 parsnip or small turnip
2½ lb lean brisket
¼ teaspoon allspice
Salt and 4 peppercorns
1 bay leaf
½ pint white wine
Water

Peel and roughly chop the carrots. Roughly chop the celery and the leaves. Remove the dirty outside leaves of the onions but keep on the golden inner skins and cut them into quarters. Peel and roughly chop the parsnip or turnip. Put the meat into a heavy saucepan and surround with the vegetables. Add the allspice, a little salt, the peppercorns and the bay leaf and pour over the white wine and enough water to cover. Bring to the boil, cover and simmer very slowly for about 2 hours until the meat is just tender.

Remove the meat, strain off the stock and measure a quarter of a pint. Add three tablespoons horseradish sauce to the stock and blend in 2 tablespoons sour cream. Heat through without boiling and serve the sauce with the meat.

Serves 6–8

Beef Olives

A delicious dish and one that can be prepared well in advance.

- 1 lb topside of beef cut into 8 very thin slices
- 8 lean rashers bacon
- 4 fresh frankfurter sausages*
- 1 teaspoon dry mustard
- 1 tablespoon olive or vegetable oil
- ¼ pint white wine
- ½ pint good stock
- 1 tablespoon tomato purée
- 2 tablespoons water
- Salt and pepper
- Pinch sage

Trim off any fat or gristle from the meat and beat well to flatten and tenderize the meat. Remove the rinds, cut the bacon rashers in half and stretch them by pulling the rashers over the back of a knife blade. Cut each frankfurter into half. Spread the meat slices with mustard, cover each slice with a piece of bacon rasher and half a frankfurter, roll up neatly and fasten with a toothpick or secure with fine white string.

Heat the oil in a heavy frying pan, add the rolls and cook over a high heat until browned on all sides. Remove the rolls with a slotted spoon. Add the wine, stock, tomato purée and water to the juices in the pan and mix well with a wooden spoon to amalgamate all the juices. Season with salt and pepper, add a pinch of sage and pour the sauce over the rolls. Return the rolls to the pan, cover tightly and cook over a very low heat for about 35–40 minutes until the meat is really tender. The rolls can be cooked in the oven in which case they should be put into a casserole dish and cooked for the same length of time in a very moderate oven (350°F, Reg 4). Remove the string or toothpicks from the rolls, arrange them on a serving dish and pour over the sauce.

The dish can be cooked in advance and heated when required.

* Fresh frankfurters, which have far more taste than tinned ones, can be bought from good delicatessen shops.

Steamed Steak and Kidney with Mushrooms

It is a pity that one of our most renowned (and rightly so) British dishes should also be horrifically weight-adding – just try enjoying a hearty meal of steak and kidney pie with its rich coating of suet pastry and then step on the scales. On the other hand there is no reason why one shouldn't enjoy the same unique flavour without the problems. Steak and kidney, gently steamed and mixed with mushrooms have all the delights of a steak and kidney pie without the obvious drawbacks. The dish takes time to make but it is worth every minute.

I use rump for this dish. It may be extravagant but I think the texture and flavour make the extra expense worthwhile. The steak and kidney can be prepared in advance and re-heated when required.

1½ lb rump or good stewing steak
1 lb lambs' kidneys
1 tablespoon flour
Salt and freshly ground black pepper
Few drops Worcestershire sauce
Pinch sage and thyme
1 bay leaf
¼ pint water or stock
¼ lb mushrooms
½ oz butter
2 tablespoons finely-chopped parsley

Trim off all the fat and gristle from the meat and cut it into 1-inch cubes. Skin the kidneys, remove any hard core and cut the meat into 1-inch cubes. Sprinkle the steak and kidneys with flour, salt and pepper and mix in the Worcestershire sauce, sage and thyme. Put the meat into a basin, pour over the water or stock, add the bay leaf and cover with grease-proof paper tied with string. Put the basin into a large saucepan and fill half-way up the sides with boiling water. Steam the steak and kidney for 3–3½ hours, replacing the water round the sides when necessary. Take off the cover, remove the bay leaf and check the seasoning.

Thinly slice the mushrooms and fry them in a little butter over a high heat for 2–3 minutes. Add them to the meat, transfer to a serving dish and sprinkle with finely-chopped parsley before serving.

Leftover Roast Beef with Miraton Sauce

One of the classic and best ways of using up the remains of a Sunday joint of roast beef which is not of the quality to serve cold.

1½ lb cold roast beef cut into thin slices
1 large onion
2 gherkins
1½ oz butter
Scant tablespoon flour
½–¾ pint stock (or water and stock cube)
1 tablespoon tomato purée
1 tablespoon red wine or cider
1 tablespoon French Dijon mustard
1 teaspoon made horseradish sauce
Salt and pepper
2 tablespoons finely-chopped parsley

Arrange the slices of beef in a very lightly greased or oiled fireproof serving dish. Peel and chop the onion and finely chop the gherkins. Melt the butter in a saucepan, add the onion and cook over a medium heat until the onion is soft and transparent. Mix in the flour and gradually blend in the stock, stirring continually over a medium high heat until the sauce is thick and smooth. Add the tomato purée, wine or cider, mustard, horseradish sauce and gherkins and season with a little salt and pepper. Simmer the sauce gently for three minutes and pour it over the meat (add a little extra stock if the sauce is too thick). Reheat in a very moderate oven (350°F, Reg 4) for 20–25 minutes. Sprinkle with parsley before serving.

Serves 4–6

Tongue with Paddington Sauce

Tongue is a useful meat since it is nearly all lean. The flavour is good, too, and lends itself to any number of spicy sauces.

1 lb cooked tongue, cut in thick slices
8 large ripe tomatoes
1 onion
1 carrot
$\frac{1}{4}$ teaspoon thyme
1 bay leaf
2 cloves garlic
2 tablespoons white wine
1 oz butter
1 teaspoon cornflour
Salt and freshly ground black pepper
1 teaspoon finely-chopped capers
2 tablespoons finely-chopped parsley

Peel the tomatoes (see page xii) and roughly chop the flesh. Peel and chop the onion. Peel and chop the carrot. Combine the tomatoes, onion, carrot, herbs and garlic in a saucepan, add the white wine and simmer gently for about 30 minutes until the carrot is soft. Remove the bay leaf and garlic and purée the mixture through a sieve, a food mill or in an electric liquidizer.

Heat the butter in a saucepan, add the cornflour and mix well, gradually blend in the tomato purée, stirring continually over a low heat until hot through. Season with salt and freshly ground black pepper. Add the slices of tongue to the sauce and heat through without stirring. Transfer to a heated serving dish and sprinkle with parsley before serving.

Gemeni Tongue

Another rather sharp dish with an interesting and rather unusual flavour.

- 4 small pickled gherkins
- 2 shallots
- 1 teaspoon French Dijon mustard
- 2 tablespoons finely-chopped parsley
- 2 tablespoons coarsely-crushed water biscuits
- ¼ pint dry white wine
- 2½ oz butter
- 1 lb cooked tongue, thinly sliced

Very finely chop the gherkins. Peel and very finely chop the shallots. Combine the gherkins, shallots, mustard, parsley, crushed biscuits and wine and season with salt and pepper. Lightly butter a shallow baking dish and spread half the mixed ingredients on the bottom. Top with the tongue slices and spread over the remaining mixture. Dot with remaining butter cut into very small pieces and bake in a very moderate oven (325°F, Reg 3) for 20 minutes.

Spiced Leg of Lamb

A leg of English lamb, young and succulent, can be one of the most delicious of all roasts but since variety is the spice of life (forgive the pun) even this traditional joint can sometimes benefit from being cooked in a new and exciting way. This recipe also has the advantage of being delicious served cold with salad, an advantage which a plain roast of lamb doesn't really share.

- 3½ lb leg lamb
- 2 cloves garlic
- 1 sprig mint
- 2 teaspoons dried rosemary
- ¼ teaspoon oregano
- 1 teaspoon ground turmeric
- 1 tablespoon coarse sea salt
- 1 teaspoon freshly ground black pepper
- 1 tablespoon olive oil
- ¼ pint red wine

Lightly prick the leg of lamb all over with a carving fork. Combine the garlic (peeled), herbs, salt and pepper in a pestle and mortar and grind to a paste with the olive oil. Rub the mixture into the leg of lamb and place the joint in a casserole or large saucepan. Cover tightly and leave in a refrigerator for at least 24 hours (preferably 48). Place the joint in a roasting dish and roast in a very moderate oven (350°F, Reg 4) for 1 hour, pour over the red wine and roast for a further ½–¾ hour (depending on whether you like your lamb pink or well-cooked) basting frequently.

Make a gravy from the juices in the pan and serve the lamb with a classical mint sauce.

Serves 5–6

Roast Leg of Lamb Provençal

Preparing lamb in this way takes a bit of extra trouble but the effort is well worth the trouble and the result is an exciting aromatic roast.

3 cloves garlic
1 tin anchovy fillets
6 black olives
3½–4 lb leg of lamb
Coarse salt and freshly ground black pepper
½ teaspoon rosemary
2 tablespoons olive oil
1 tin tomatoes (15 oz)
¼ pint red wine

Peel the garlic and cut the cloves into thin slivers. Soak the drained anchovy fillets in milk for five minutes, drain well, pat dry on kitchen paper and cut into small snippets. Cut the flesh of the black olives into thin slivers. Rub the leg of lamb with coarse salt and freshly ground black pepper and make incisions, about a quarter of an inch in depth, all over the surface, with a sharp pointed knife. Press the pieces of garlic, anchovy and olive into these incisions, sprinkle with rosemary and pour over the olive oil.

Roast the lamb in a moderate oven for 1 hour. Pour over the tomatoes and red wine and continue to roast for a further half to three-quarters of an hour (depending on how pink you like your meat) basting frequently. Place the lamb on a heated serving dish and keep warm. Add the stock to the tomatoes and juices in the pan and mix well. Purée the sauce through a sieve, reheat and serve separately.

Serves 6

Rack of Lamb

One of the very nicest ways to cook and serve lamb but it must be made with fresh English lamb and not those rather dead frozen joints some butchers like to sell you.

1 rack of lamb from the best end neck (2–3 cutlets per serving depending on the size)
Juice 1 lemon
2 tablespoons olive oil
2 tablespoons fine dry breadcrumbs
2 teaspoons rosemary or a sprig of fresh rosemary
Salt and freshly ground black pepper

Ask your butcher to remove the skin from the rack and to chine off the fat from the top of the bones (or do this yourself; it isn't as tricky to do as it sounds). Combine the lemon juice with the olive oil and season with salt and pepper. Brush the rack with this mixture and sprinkle the fat side with dry breadcrumbs. Sprinkle over the rosemary and roast in a moderate oven (375°F, Reg 5) for about 30 minutes, basting frequently, until well-browned but still pink in the inside.

Divide into cutlets at the table and serve with mint sauce.

Ourika Lamb

Turmeric was a spice I seldom used until I went to Marrakech. Since then I use it constantly, and very successfully, especially in lamb dishes. This is a typical example; fragrant, spicy, sharp and delicious. Serve it with one of the rice dishes on pages 168–71.

1½ lb lean lamb from the leg or shoulder
2 cloves garlic
1½ teaspoons turmeric
1 teaspoon cardomon seeds
4 tablespoons olive oil
Juice 1 lemon
6 oz small button mushrooms
1 small tin tomatoes
1 tablespoon finely-chopped parsley
1 carton yoghurt (5 fl oz)
Salt and pepper

Cut the lamb into 1-inch cubes. Remove skin of cardomon seeds. Peel the garlic and place the cloves in a pestle and mortar with the turmeric and the cardomon seeds. Pound the mixture to a smooth paste and blend in the olive oil and lemon juice. Marinate the lamb in the sauce for at least four hours. Drain off and reserve the marinade. Heat a frying pan, add the lamb and cook over a fast heat until brown on all sides. Add the mushrooms, tomatoes and parsley and pour over the marinade. Season with salt and pepper. Cook over a low heat for 30–45 minutes until the meat is tender. Blend in the yoghurt and heat through without boiling.

Serve at once.

Lamb Casserole with Runner Beans

1½ lb lean lamb from the leg or shoulder
2 onions
1 lb runner beans
2 tablespoons olive oil
¼ pint hot water
Salt and freshly ground black pepper

Cut the lamb into 1-inch cubes. Peel and finely chop the

onions. Remove the tops and tails of the runner beans and any tough strings from the sides. Cut the beans into 1-inch pieces. Heat the olive oil in a flameproof casserole. Add the onions and lamb and cook over a high heat, stirring every now and then, for 15 minutes. Add the beans, pour over the water and season with salt and pepper. Bring to the boil, cover and simmer gently for about 30 minutes until the meat is really tender.

Grilled Lamb Cutlets

Few things can beat plump English lamb cutlets, trimmed of all their fat and cooked under a hot grill until the outside is nicely browned and the inside still a succulent pink. Allow 2–3 cutlets, depending on size (I like them as small as possible) and keep the side dishes plain and simple.

8–12 small lamb cutlets	Salt and freshly ground black pepper
Olive oil	Juice ½ lemon
1 teaspoon dried rosemary	

Trim off the fat from the cutlets and chine the top of the bone (use a sharp knife to cut all the skin and flesh round one inch of the top of the bone to make a neat end). Brush the meat with a very little olive oil, sprinkle with rosemary and season with freshly ground black pepper. Grill under a high heat for 3–4 minutes on each side until well browned. Season with a little salt and lemon juice and serve at once.

Kasbah Kidneys

Until I discovered this recipe, kidneys were not one of my favourite dishes; I always found them too rich and sweet and I never could understand why people made them richer and sweeter by serving them in sauces heavily laced with sherry and cream. Discovering this recipe changed all that. Marinating the kidneys with herbs, spices and plenty of lemon juice takes away that rich sweetness and gives them such a flavour that they don't need the addition of a sauce.

2 cloves garlic
Juice 1½ lemons
3 tablespoons olive oil
1 teaspoon crushed cardomon seeds
½ teaspoon turmeric
½ teaspoon rosemary
6 lambs' kidneys
½ lb firm button mushrooms
Salt and freshly ground black pepper

Crush the garlic cloves or pass them through a garlic press. Combine the lemon juice, olive oil, cardomon seeds, turmeric, rosemary and garlic, season with salt and pepper and mix well. Remove the skins of the kidneys, cut each one in half and remove the hard core. Cut the kidneys into 1-inch cubes. Trim off the stalks of the button mushrooms and add them to the marinade with the kidneys. Mix gently to avoid breaking up the mushrooms and leave to stand in a cool place for at least two hours.

Thread the mushrooms and kidneys on 4 large or 8 small skewers, brush them with any marinade which has not been absorbed and grill them under a hot flame for about five to eight minutes, turning frequently (the kidneys should still be a little pink inside).

Serve with rice and a salad.

Brandied Kidneys

4 spring onions
8 oz firm button mushrooms
3 tablespoons olive oil
2 tablespoons flour
½ pint chicken stock (or water and stock cube)
6 lambs' kidneys
1 tablespoon lemon juice
1 oz butter
2 tablespoons brandy
Salt and freshly ground black pepper

Roughly chop the spring onions. Thinly slice the mushrooms. Heat the olive oil in a saucepan, add the onions and mushrooms and cook for 3 minutes over a medium heat. Blend in the flour and gradually add the stock, stirring lightly over a medium heat. Season with salt and pepper, bring to the boil and simmer gently for 20 minutes.

Remove the skin of the kindeys and cut each one in half. Cut out the tough white core and brush with lemon juice. Leave to stand for 15 minutes. Heat the butter in a frying pan, add the kidneys and cook over a high heat, stirring every now and then, for 3 minutes. Pour over the brandy, heat through and set alight. Remove the kidneys from the heat as soon as the flames have died down. Add the kidneys to the sauce, check the seasoning and heat through if necessary.

Tommy's Dill Pickled Kidneys

Tommy is an ideal guest. On a careful diet with a troublesome weight problem, but nevertheless devoted to good food, this dish tickled his fancy, so I called it after him.

6 lambs' kidneys
Flour
2 onions
1 green pepper
4 oz dill pickled cucumber
2 tablespoons olive oil
1 tablespoon cucumber liquid
¼ pint stock
3 tablespoons sour cream
Salt
Pinch cayenne pepper

Remove the skin from the kidneys and cut each one in half. Remove the tough core and dice the kidneys. Lightly coat the kidney pieces in flour seasoned with salt and a little cayenne pepper. Peel and finely chop the onions. Peel and finely chop the pepper and cut the dill pickled cucumber into small dice. Heat the olive oil in a frying pan, add the kidneys and cook over a high heat, turning frequently, until well-browned on all sides. Remove the kidneys with a slotted spoon and add the onions and pepper to the juices in the pan. Cook over a medium heat for 5 minutes, stirring constantly, until the onions are soft and transparent. Blend in the juice from the pickled cucumber and the stock, mix well and simmer for 5 minutes. Add the kidney and chopped cucumber and continue to simmer for a further five minutes. Check seasoning and blend in the sour cream.

Heat through without boiling.

Hungarian Pork Tenderloin

Pork is a fatty meat on the whole; one of the exceptions is the tenderloin, a sweet, lean meat with a special taste to it. Trim off any fat from the tenderloins to avoid any temptation.

2 tenderloins
1 tablespoon paprika pepper
1 large onion
½ oz butter
1 tablespoon olive oil
1 medium tin tomatoes
1 tablespoon tomato purée
2 tablespoons sherry
1 teaspoon sage
Pinch basil
Salt and pepper
2 tablespoons sour cream

Cut the tenderloins into ½-inch thick slices. Place the slices on a piece of greaseproof paper, cover with a second piece of paper and beat with a mallet or rolling pin until thin and almost doubled in size. Season with paprika. Peel and thinly slice the onion and divide into rings. Heat the butter and olive oil until smoking in a large heavy frying pan, add the pork slices and cook over a high heat until browned on both sides. Drain on kitchen paper, transfer to a heated serving dish and keep warm.

Add the onion to the juices in the pan and cook over a moderate heat until the onion is soft and golden – about 5 minutes. Add the tinned tomatoes, herbs and tomato purée, season with salt and pepper and blend in the sherry. Simmer gently, stirring occasionally, for 10 minutes. Return the pork to the pan, stir in the sour cream and heat through without boiling.

VEAL

Some cuts of veal provide the leanest meat available and are therefore ideal for the weight watcher. Unfortunately, the better cuts tend to be pricey and in some parts of the country are very difficult to get. In Cornwall, where I live, veal is like gold dust and seldom to be found. When I get the chance to buy some, I grab the opportunity.

The leanest cut, and also the most economical, is the fillet cut from the top of the leg. Often, slices of fillet (escalopes) are coated in egg and breadcrumbs and fried or the veal is served with a rich creamy sauce but there are many alternative, non-fattening ways of cooking the meat which can be delicious.

Vitello Selina

4 escalopes of veal
Flour
2 oz firm button mushrooms
½ oz butter
1 tablespoon olive oil
1 carton yoghurt (5 fl oz)
¼ pint white wine
Pinch paprika pepper
Salt and pepper
2 tablespoons finely-chopped parsley

Lightly coat the veal in seasoned flour. Thinly slice the mushrooms. Heat the butter and olive oil in a frying pan. Add the veal and cook over a medium heat until golden brown on each side. Remove on to a heated serving dish and keep warm. Add the mushrooms to the juices in the pan and cook for 3 minutes. Blend in the yoghurt and wine, season with a pinch of paprika and heat through without boiling. Pour the sauce over the meat and sprinkle with finely-chopped parsley before serving.

Veal Chops with Wine and Herbs

8 veal chops
Salt and freshly ground black pepper
$1\frac{1}{2}$ oz butter
1 tablespoon olive oil
$\frac{1}{4}$ pint dry white wine
$\frac{1}{4}$ pint water
1 tablespoon finely-chopped chives
1 tablespoon finely-chopped parsley
2 tablespoons sour cream

Cut any fat off the chops and season them with freshly ground black pepper. Heat the butter and olive oil in a heavy frying pan, add the chops and brown quickly on both sides. Pour off any excess fat, sprinkle the chops with salt and pour over the wine and water. Cover and simmer very gently for 20 minutes. Mix in the chives and parsley and simmer for a further 10 minutes.

Remove the chops and arrange them on a heated serving dish. Add the sour cream to the sauce in the pan and mix well over a low heat until smooth.

Stuffed Loin of Veal

1 onion
$\frac{1}{4}$ teaspoon rosemary
2 lean rashers bacon
2 oz grated cheddar cheese
Grated rind $\frac{1}{2}$ orange
3 lb boned loin of veal
$\frac{1}{8}$ pint olive oil
1 glass white wine
Juice 1 orange
Salt and freshly ground black pepper

Peel and finely chop the onion. Pound the rosemary to a powder in a mortar with a pestle. Remove the rinds of the bacon and finely mince the flesh. Combine the bacon, cheese, chopped onion, rosemary and orange rind and season with a little salt and pepper. Spread the stuffing on the boned side of the veal and roll up tightly. Tie with string and place the meat in a roasting dish. Brush the joint with olive oil, cover lightly with tinfoil and roast in a very moderate oven (350°F, Reg 4) for 1 hour, basting occasionally. Pour over the wine and orange juice and continue to cook for a further ½ hour.

Transfer the meat to a heated serving dish, strain off the juices from the pan and remove any fat from the surface. Cut the meat into thin slices, pour over the sauce and serve at once.

Serves 6

Grilled Veal Chops with Sharp Fruit Sauce

A simple way of cooking the chops which seals in all the natural flavours.

8 thin veal cutlets
1 tablespoon olive oil
Juice ½ lemon
Pinch rosemary
Pinch sage
2 eating apples
1 tablespoon water
½ oz butter
½ orange
Salt and freshly ground black pepper

Remove the fat from the cutlets, season them with salt and pepper and brush with the olive oil mixed with the lemon juice. Grill the chops under a moderately low flame for 8–10 minutes on each side. Peel, core and chop the apples. Remove the peel and membrane from the orange and chop the flesh. Combine the apple, water, orange, sage and rosemary in a saucepan, season with salt and pepper, bring to the boil and simmer gently for 20 minutes. Purée the fruit through a sieve, a food mill or in an electric liquidizer.

Serve the chops with the fruit sauce.

Baked Liver with Tart Apples

The rather sweet taste of liver makes this combination ideal; a dish that is highly nutritional, economical and popular with all the family. Make sure the liver is cut into very thin slices.

1 lb liver
3 cooking apples
2 onions
4 rashers lean bacon
½ pint hot stock (or water and chicken or beef stock cube)
½ tablespoon paprika pepper
Salt and freshly ground black pepper

Cut the liver into very thin slices and remove any tough fibres or membranes. Peel and thickly slice the apples. Peel and chop the onions. Cut the bacon into ½-inch-wide strips. Place the liver in a lightly-oiled baking dish, season with a little salt and pepper and top with the mixed onions and apples. Season lightly and cover with the bacon rashers. Pour over the stock and bake in a very moderate oven (350°F Reg 4) for 25 minutes or until liver is tender.

Charlestown Liver

A liver stew cooked on top of the stove and flavoured with a combination of vegetables.

1 onion
1 clove garlic
2 carrots
3 stalks celery
3 leeks
2 ripe tomatoes
1 lb calves' or lambs' liver
Flour
3 tablespoons olive oil
1 cup stock (or water and beef stock cube)
1 tablespoon dry sherry (optional)
Pinch rosemary and oregano
Salt and pepper

Peel and finely chop the onion. Squeeze the garlic through a garlic press. Peel and finely chop the carrots. Thinly slice the celery and wash and thinly slice the leeks. Peel and roughly chop the tomatoes. Cut the liver into very thin slices and remove any tough fibres and membrane. Dust the liver lightly with seasoned flour. Heat the olive oil in a large frying pan, add the liver and cook over a high heat until well browned on both sides but still pink in the centre. Remove the liver, add the onion, garlic, carrots, celery, leeks and tomatoes, and mix well to amalgamate the juices in the pan. Cook the vegetables over a medium heat until soft. Pour over the stock, add the herbs, cover and simmer gently for 10 minutes. Add the liver, check the seasoning, mix in the sherry and heat through.

Calves' Liver Venetian Style

If you go to Venice and don't sample this classic dish, you will miss out on something special. To be successful the liver must be cut into almost wafer thin slices and it is best to buy the liver in one piece and do this yourself, using a really sharp knife.

1 lb calves' liver
2 onions
2 tablespoons olive oil
Salt and pepper
1 tablespoon very finely-chopped parsley
Pinch of dried sage (or 2 leaves fresh sage, finely-chopped)

Cut the liver into wafer-thin slices and then in finger-sized pieces. Peel and very thinly slice the onions and divide into rings. Heat the oil in a large frying pan, add the onions and cook over a high heat until the onions are well browned. Add the liver and cook for 2 minutes, moving the pieces around the pan to ensure they cook evenly. Season with salt and pepper, mix in the parsley and sage, cook for a further ½ minute and serve at once. Do not overcook.

Sweetbreads en Brochette

The taste of sweetbreads is a gentle flavour, similar to that of gently poached chicken breasts. They are most valuable to the slimmer as they contain virtually no fat, are a reasonable price and can be served in countless different ways. Some books will tell you that sweetbreads, like brains, should be blanched before being used for composite dishes; I find this unnecessary and certainly the original blanching detracts from their special taste.

1 lb sweetbreads
1 egg
1 tablespoon lemon juice
Crushed water biscuits
3 rashers very thinly-cut lean bacon
½ lb button mushrooms
1 green pepper
2 tablespoons olive oil
Salt and pepper
Paprika pepper

Cut the sweetbreads into 1-inch pieces. Combine the egg and lemon juice and mix well. Dip the sweetbreads into the egg mixture and then lightly coat with crushed water biscuit crumbs. Remove the rind from the bacon, cut the rashers into 1-inch wide strips and roll up tightly. Remove the stalks from the mushrooms. Remove the core and seeds from the pepper and cut the flesh into 1-inch squares.

Divide the ingredients on four skewers, alternating the sweetbreads and bacon with the vegetables. Brush with olive oil, season with salt and a generous sprinkling of paprika and grill under a medium heat for 15 minutes, turning occasionally and basting with the juices in the pan. Sprinkle with a little salt and serve with a grapefruit and watercress salad (see page 184).

Sweetbreads with Bacon

This is such a simple dish and yet I know a number of people who will go especially to one of the best restaurants in London in order to enjoy it.

1½ lb sweetbreads
Crushed water biscuits
8 very thin rashers bacon
1 tablespoon olive oil
½ oz butter
Salt, pepper and paprika
Lemon wedges
Watercress

Divide the sweetbreads into 1½-inch pieces. Dip each piece in water biscuit crumbs. Remove the rinds of the bacon rashers. Cook the bacon in the olive oil over a high heat until crisp, drain on kitchen paper and keep warm. Add the butter to the juice in the pan, heat through and add the sweetbreads. Cook them over a high heat, turning every now and then, until golden brown. Lower the heat and cook for a further ten minutes. Remove the sweetbreads and arrange them on a serving dish with the bacon rashers. Garnish with lemon wedges and watercress.

Maidenwell Sweetbreads

A slightly richer dish but still not too heavy for the purposes of this book.

1 lb sweetbreads
¼ lb ham
1 green or red pepper
1½ oz butter
1 tablespoon olive oil
1 tablespoon flour
¼ pint milk
¼ pint chicken stock (or water and stock cube)
Salt and freshly ground black pepper
2 egg yolks
2 tablespoons finely-crushed water biscuits
1½ oz finely-grated cheddar cheese

Divide the sweetbreads into 1-inch pieces. Chop the ham. Remove the core and seeds of the pepper and chop the flesh. Blanch the pepper in boiling, salted water for 5 minutes and drain well. Heat 1 oz butter with 1 tablespoon olive oil in a saucepan, add the sweetbreads and cook over a medium high heat for 3 minutes. Remove the sweetbreads with a slotted spoon. Blend the flour into the juices in the pan and gradually add the milk and stock, stirring continually until the sauce is thick and smooth. Add the sweetbreads, ham and peppers, season with salt and pepper, cover and simmer for 15 minutes.

Add a little of the sauce to the egg yolks and mix well. Blend the egg yolks into the remaining sauce and stir gently until the mixture is slightly thickened and shiny. Transfer to a baking dish and top with the biscuit crumbs mixed with the grated cheese. Brown quickly under a hot grill and serve at once.

Calves' Brains with Onions and Mushrooms

The taste of brains is an acquired taste and one of which I am particularly fond. Usually, they are served with toast, croûtons or in pastry or bread cases and cooked with heavy, rich sauces to disguise their taste. This always seems a waste to me – either you like brains enough to eat them or you choose alternative fare. In this recipe, they are cooked in a light sauce with vegetables, then thickened with egg yolks and given a light flavouring of lemon juice.

1 lb calves' brains
8 very small onions
¼ lb firm button mushrooms
1 oz butter
1 tablespoon flour
½ pint hot chicken stock
2 egg yolks
½ tablespoon lemon juice
Salt and freshly ground black pepper
1 tablespoon very finely-chopped parsley

Wash the brains and soak them for 1 hour in warm water. Remove the arteries and skin membranes and plunge into boiling, salted water. Cook for 15 minutes, then rinse in cold water, drain well and leave to cool. Cut the brains into bite-sized pieces. Peel the onions and thinly slice the mushrooms. Blanch the mushrooms in boiling salted water for 3 minutes and drain well.

Melt the butter in a saucepan, add the flour and mix well. Gradually blend in the chicken stock, stirring continually over a medium heat until the sauce is thick and smooth. Add the onions and mushrooms, season with salt and pepper and simmer very gently for 30 minutes. Add the brains and cook for a further 15 minutes or until the onions are tender. Remove the brains, onions and mushrooms with a slotted spoon and arrange them on a heated serving dish. Beat the egg yolks with the lemon juice and add a little of the hot sauce. Mix until smooth and then add to the remaining sauce, stirring all the time over a low heat until the sauce is thick and smooth. Stir in the parsley, check the seasoning and pour the sauce over the brains.

Casserole of Rabbit

A real huntsman's dish which should be made over an open camp fire but still tastes delicious if cooked in a more conventional manner.

1 skinned and cleaned rabbit
2 tablespoons flour
Salt and freshly ground black pepper
1 large onion
4 oz mushrooms
¼ lb fat bacon
2 tablespoons brandy
1¼ pints dry white wine
Rind ½ lemon
2 sprigs parsley
8 peppercorns
2 sticks celery
2 egg yolks

Cut off the legs of the rabbit and divide the back into 4 pieces. Mix the flour with a little salt and pepper and coat the rabbit with the seasoned flour. Peel and finely chop the onions. Thinly slice the mushrooms. Remove the rinds from the bacon, and cut the rashers into 2-inch wide strips. Cook the rinds and bacon, without extra fat, over a medium high heat until most of the fat has dissolved. Discard the rinds and remove the bacon pieces with a slotted spoon. Add the rabbit joints to the hot bacon fat and cook over a high heat until brown on all sides. Remove the joints and add the onions to the juices in the pan. Cook the onions over a low heat until soft and transparent, add the mushrooms and cook for a further 2 minutes. Return the rabbit joints and bacon to the pan, heat the brandy, pour it over the rabbit and set it alight. Shake the pan until the flames have died down. Pour over the wine, heat through and transfer the ingredients to a fireproof casserole. Add the parsley, peppercorns and celery, cover tightly and simmer over a low heat for 1 hour or until the rabbit is really tender.

Discard the celery stalks and parsley and strain off the sauce. Arrange the rabbit, onions and mushrooms on a heated serving dish and keep warm. Beat the egg yolks until well mixed, add a little of the sauce and beat until smooth. Add the yolk mixture to the remaining sauce and cook over a very low heat, stirring continually, until the sauce thickens slightly. Check the seasoning and pour the sauce over the rabbit. Serve at once.

Baked Rabbit with Herbs and Sour Cream

Rabbits have tender and tasty flesh with virtually no fat. If cooked in an interesting way, they make a delightful meal.

1 skinned and cleaned rabbit
2 tablespoons flour
Salt and freshly ground
black pepper
3 onions
1 carton sour cream (5 fl oz)
¼ pint stock or water
Pinch tarragon and thyme
1 tablespoon olive oil
1 oz butter

Cut off the legs of the rabbit and cut the back into 4 pieces. Mix the flour with salt and pepper and lightly coat the rabbit pieces with the seasoned flour. Peel and thinly slice thc onions. Combine the sour cream and stock or water, add the herbs, season lightly and mix well. Heat the butter and oil in a frying pan until smoking. Add the rabbit and brown quickly on all sides. Drain the joints on kitchen paper and transfer to a casserole. Arrange the onion slices over the rabbit and pour over the sour cream sauce. Cover with a layer of foil and a tight-fitting lid and cook in a slow oven (300°F, Reg 2) for 1½ hours until tender.

Delicious chicken and poultry dishes to satisfy the appetite without ruining the waistline

Although, like everything else, poultry has risen in price during the last year it is still very economical and competitive with most of the more expensive meat dishes. There is also the advantage that the giblets and carcass make a good stock base for soup and the flesh lends itself to a wide variety of both hot and cold dishes.

Factory farming and artificial foodstuffs have unfortunately led to the deterioration of most chickens these days and, where possible, I would recommend buying your poultry from a really reputable source and paying a little extra to get a fresh, not frozen, bird (the trouble about frozen poultry is that there is seldom any guarantee as to how long it has been kept in the freezer).

Being nearly all lean meat, chickens make good eating for the figure-conscious, especially if they are boiled and the fatty skin is removed before eating.

Sozzled Chicken

1 roasting chicken
3 tablespoons olive oil
Salt and freshly ground black pepper
Pinch cayenne pepper
1 large onion
2 cloves garlic
½ pint stock (or chicken stock cube and water)
¼ pint dry white wine
2 oz ground almonds
2 egg yolks
2 tablespoons brandy
1 tablespoon finely-chopped parsley

Divide the chicken into eight joints and season them with salt, freshly ground black pepper and a pinch of cayenne. Heat the olive oil until smoking in a large heavy frying pan. Add the chicken and cook over a high heat until the chicken is golden brown on all sides. Peel and finely chop the onion. Peel and crush the garlic. Add the onion and garlic to the chicken and cook over a medium low heat for five minutes, stirring to prevent sticking. Pour over the water or stock and the wine, season with salt and simmer gently for about 30 minutes or until the chicken is tender.

Combine the ground almonds, egg yolks and brandy and mix to a smooth paste. Remove the chicken pieces and onion onto a heated serving dish with a slotted spoon and keep warm. Blend the paste into the juices in the pan and mix well, simmer for 10 minutes, pour the sauce over the chicken and sprinkle with finely chopped parsley.

Serves 6

Spring Chicken with Gruyère

I find this the best way to deal with those rather tasteless but very tender little birds.

2 spring chickens, halved
Juice 1 lemon
Salt and freshly ground black pepper
1½ oz butter, melted
3 oz coarsely grated Gruyère cheese

Brush the chicken halves on both sides with lemon juice and season with salt and plenty of freshly ground black pepper. Brush with melted butter and grill under a medium heat, basting frequently for 10 minutes on each side. Cover the breast sides of the chickens with grated cheese, return to the grill and cook until the cheese melts, bubbles and is golden brown.

Serve with a watercress salad.

Grilled Baby Chickens

The flavour of these little birds isn't much to write home about but they do have the most succulent tenderness. Cooked in this way and served straight from the grill they make an excellent dish.

4 small poussins
Juice 1½ lemons
1 teaspoon rosemary
Salt and freshly ground black pepper
Pinch of paprika
1 oz melted butter

Using a very sharp knife, cut each bird down the breast, split open, lay them on a board and beat lightly to flatten. Trim off the wing tips and the feet. Combine the lemon juice, rosemary and seasonings and brush the mixture all over the birds. Dribble over the melted butter and grill under a medium hot flame for 20–30 minutes, basting frequently, until the birds are cooked and a rich golden brown.

Serve with a watercress salad.

Sylvia's Chicken Delight

½ lb cooked chicken cut in thin slices
¼ lb Gruyère cheese
8 thin slices ham
1 clove garlic
1 small onion
3 cardomon seeds
¼ teaspoon turmeric
¼ teaspoon cummin seeds
2 tablespoons olive oil
Pinch sugar
1 medium tin tomatoes
1 tablespoon dry Vermouth
Salt and pepper

Cut cheese into thin slices. Arrange chicken and cheese in centre of ham slices, roll up neatly and arrange in a shallow, lightly-greased baking dish. Peel and crush garlic. Peel and finely chop onion. Remove skin of cardomon seeds and crush spices with a pestle in a mortar. Heat oil, add garlic and onion and cook over medium heat until onion is transparent. Add sugar, spices, tomatoes and vermouth and cook for 15 minutes. Season with salt and pepper and pour sauce over ham rolls. Cover with tin foil and bake in a moderate oven (375°F, Reg 5) for 20 minutes.

Simmered Chicken with Lemon Tarragon Sauce

Boiled chicken may not sound like any great cop but this dish has a tenderness and subtlety about it which is hard to beat, with the added advantage of producing enough juices to make the base of a nourishing stock. The sauce is smooth and memorable.

1 chicken (about 3 lb)
1 large onion
1 clove garlic
2 carrots
1 stick celery
1 chicken stock cube
Bouquet garni
8 black peppercorns
½ lemon
¼ pint white wine

The sauce
1 oz butter
1 tablespoon flour
½ pint stock
2 teaspoons tarragon
2 teaspoons lemon juice
2 egg yolks
2 cartons sour cream (10 fl oz)
Salt and freshly ground black pepper

Place the chicken, with the gizzard, heart and neck, in a saucepan (reserve the liver for adding to a soup as a garnish). Add, the onion, garlic and carrots, peeled and roughly chopped, the celery stalk cut into three, the stock cube, bouquet garni, peppercorns, lemon and white wine. Pour over enough water to cover the bird, bring slowly to the boil, stir to dissolve the stock cube and simmer very slowly for 1 hour or until the chicken is tender. Remove the bird and strain off ½ pint stock (reserve remaining stock and vegetables to re-boil with the chicken carcass to make a stronger stock for soup). Leave the chicken to cool, then carve, cutting the breast into thin slices and dividing up the joints. Arrange the chicken on a shallow serving dish.

Melt the butter in a saucepan, add the flour and mix well. Gradually blend in the stock, stirring continually until the sauce comes to the boil and is thick and smooth. Add the tarragon and lemon juice and simmer gently for five minutes. Mix the egg yolks with the sour cream. Remove the sauce from the heat, beat in the cream and egg yolk mixture, season with salt and pepper if necessary and pour the sauce over the chicken. Heat through in a very moderate oven (350°F, Reg 4) for about 15 minutes. Garnish with finely-chopped parsley or a little chopped fresh tarragon.

Serve with 'Slim Jim Rice' (see page 168).

Stuffed Chicken Thighs

Packets of fresh chicken thighs, wings and drumsticks can be bought from supermarkets and I find these invaluable for making a good many interesting and unusual dishes at a reasonable cost. This particular dish is one I am especially proud of and which I always find very popular.

Garam Masala is an Indian mixture of ground spices, widely used in the East. It has a lighter and more subtle taste than curry powder and can be found in most good delicatessen shops. If Garam Masala is not available, curry powder can be used as a substitute.

8 chicken thighs
2 onions
1 carrot
1 green pepper
1 celery stalk
1 tablespoon olive oil
1 teaspoon Garam Masala
2 tablespoons tomato purée
1 cooking apple
Salt and freshly ground black pepper

Using a sharp knife, make a slit down the side of the chicken thighs and neatly cut out the bones. Place the bones in a saucepan and cook over a high heat until they are lightly browned. Cover the bones with water and add one onion (roughly chopped) and the carrot (roughly chopped). Season with salt and pepper, bring to the boil and simmer for about thirty minutes to make a rich stock.

Finely chop the remaining onion. Remove the core and seeds of the green pepper and finely chop the flesh. Very thinly slice the celery stalk.

Heat the oil in a small frying pan, add the onion, pepper and celery and cook over a low heat until the vegetables are soft. Stir in the Garam Masala and the tomato purée. Spread the stuffing over the cut side of the chicken thighs and roll up as neatly as possible. Arrange the thighs in a baking dish and pour over the stock. Cook uncovered, in a hot oven (450°F, Reg 8) for 15 minutes.

Peel and core the apple and cut into thick slices. Arrange the slices in between the chicken pieces, baste with some of the juices and continue to cook in a hot oven for a further 20 minutes until the chicken is golden brown and tender.

Dimbodie Quail

These small, succulent, little birds are rapidly becoming more popular, and more readily available, in this country. Although classed as a game bird, they should be eaten fresh and not hung as with woodcock or snipe. Allow two birds for each serving and have finger bowls on the table as one inevitably ends up by dismembering them with the help of fingers.

Vine leaves can be bought in tins from most good delicatessen shops and should be carefully rinsed in cold water and then patted dry with kitchen paper before being wrapped round the birds.

4 oz rice
Stock
2 tablespoons sultanas
½ oz butter
Salt and pepper
Pinch cayenne pepper
8 quails
8 rashers bacon
8 vine leaves
4 oz dripping

Cook rice in boiling stock until tender. Drain off excess liquid and stir in sultanas, ½ oz butter and seasoning. Leave to cool.

Pluck, draw and wipe the quail. Stuff cavities with the rice mixture and wrap each bird in a rasher of bacon. Season with a little salt, pepper and a pinch of cayenne and then parcel each neatly in a vine leaf. Heat dripping in a roasting tin, put in the birds and roast in a moderate oven (375°F, Reg 5) for 35 minutes, basting frequently.

Serve with spinach in sour cream and a salad.

Pigeon Delegado

Roast pigeon can be delicious but only if the birds cooked this way are really young and tender. Older birds should be stewed or casseroled.

Choose small, plump birds with finely-grained flesh. Check with your poulterer that they are suitable for roasting.

4 oz chicken livers
1 shallot
4 anchovy fillets
4 juniper berries
4 oz butter
1 teaspoon thyme
Salt and pepper
4 young pigeons
1 tablespoon redcurrant jelly
1 carton sour cream (5 fl oz)

Finely chop chicken livers. Peel and finely chop shallot. Finely chop or mince anchovy fillets. Crush juniper berries. Melt 2 oz butter in a frying pan. Add chicken livers, shallot, anchovies, juniper berries and thyme and cook over a low heat for three minutes. Season with salt and pepper and stuff the birds with this mixture.

Season remaining butter with salt and pepper and rub it well into the skin of the pigeons. Roast the birds in a moderately hot oven (400°F, Reg 6) for 35 minutes, until tender, basting frequently.

Mix the redcurrant jelly and cream together and heat through without boiling. Season with salt and pepper and pour over the birds just before serving.

The cold table with recipes that offer no temptations

Beef is unfortunately one of the most expensive meats on the market these days and the time when you could happily fall back on a traditional roast to meet any situation is over, but, on the other hand, the better cuts of beef are wonderfully lean and therefore a boon to the weight-watcher. One good compromise between watching cost and weight is to settle for a roast which can be served cold and which will therefore stretch far further than a hot joint. Cut the meat into wafer thin slices and serve it with a selection of salads to make a perfect summer meal. Trim off all fat before serving.

If beef is at a premium, other roast meats can equally well be served cold with the same advantages. Cold lamb, for instance, is very underrated; if the meat is well-flavoured with rosemary, garlic and lemon juice during cooking the flesh is just as good when the roast has cooled providing it is, again, cut into very thin slices and served with an interesting selection of salads. Veal, also expensive and not so easy to buy in this country, is frequently improved by cooling after cooking and, like any other cold meat, will stretch far further and be much easier to carve.

Cold Roast Fillet of Beef

3 lb fillet of beef
2 tablespoons dripping
Salt and freshly ground black pepper
3 tablespoons brandy

Trim the fillet of all sinews and fat and rub the flesh with freshly ground black pepper. Melt the dripping in a baking dish, add the meat and cook over a high heat for 6 minutes until the meat is well browned on all sides. Warm the brandy in a small saucepan, pour it over the meat, set it alight and continue to cook the meat on top of the stove, shaking the pan, until the flames die out. Sprinkle with a little salt, transfer the fillet to a moderately hot oven (400°F, Reg 6) and roast for a further 15–20 minutes, basting frequently.

Place the meat on a clean dish, pour over the juices from the pan and leave to get completely cold before carving.

Serves 6–8

Beef Salad with Hard-boiled Eggs

One of the nicest ways to use up the remains of a tender, red rare, joint of beef. Remove any fat from the meat and cut it into wafer-thin slices.

- 1 lb cold roast beef
- 3 hard-boiled eggs
- 2 spring onions
- 6 radishes
- 3 tablespoons olive oil
- 1 tablespoon white wine vinegar
- 1 teaspoon French Dijon mustard
- ½ tablespoon finely-chopped parsley
- 1 teaspoon finely-chopped capers
- Salt and freshly ground black pepper

Arrange the beef in a shallow serving dish. Shell and slice the eggs and arrange them on top of the meat. Finely chop the spring onions and thinly slice the radishes. Combine the olive oil, vinegar, salt, pepper and mustard in a screw-top jar and shake to mix well. Mix in the spring onions, parsley and capers and pour the dressing over the eggs and meat. Garnish with slices of radish and chill well before serving.

Cold Fillet of Beef with Mustard Mayonnaise

A fillet of beef is expensive and for many purposes less full of flavour than one of the other good cuts, such as entrecote or rump. This dish, however, because it is served cold, stretches a long way, and as a summer luncheon dish for a party is hard to beat. The secret lies in leaving the meat to get really cold before you carve it and then cutting it in paper-thin slices on a wooden chopping board, using a razor-sharp knife. The meat must be really rare to bring out the full taste.

1 fillet of beef cut from the thick end (about 2½–3 lb)
Freshly ground black pepper
3 rashers really fat bacon
½ pint home-made mayonnaise (see page 194)
2 tablespoons French Dijon mustard
Watercress for garnishing

A good butcher will have trimmed off all the fat and muscle from the fillet. If this has not been done, pare off any fat and sinew from the meat and press it into a neat shape. Place the meat in a roasting tin, season it with freshly ground black pepper and place the fat bacon over the top. Roast the fillet in a pre-heated hot oven (400°F, Reg 6) for 10 minutes to seal in the juices, then lower the heat to very moderate (325°F, Reg 3) and continue to cook for a further 1–1¼ hours, basting frequently. Remove the bacon, place the meat in a casserole dish, pour over the juices from the pan and press it with a plate and a heavy weight. Leave the meat to get completely cold and then cut into the *thinnest* possible slices. Arrange the meat on a serving dish and garnish with a little watercress. Beat the mustard into the mayonnaise and dribble the sauce over the meat from a spoon in a criss-cross pattern.

Serve with a selection of salads.

Serves 8

Cold Spiced Topside of Beef

3 lb topside of beef with fat removed
1 clove garlic
1 pint orange juice
½ pint tomato juice
1 tablespoon olive oil
½ teaspoon allspice
½ teaspoon chilli powder or a few drops Tabasco sauce
Salt and freshly ground black pepper

Place the meat in a bowl. Crush the garlic clove and combine with the orange juice, tomato juice, olive oil, allspice and chilli, season with salt and pepper and pour the marinade over the meat. Leave in a refrigerator for at least six hours, turning the meat every now and then to make sure it is well marinated.

Remove the meat from the marinade and roast it in a very moderate oven (325°F, Reg 3) for 45 minutes. Pour over remaining marinade and continue to cook for a further 30 minutes, basting frequently with the juices in the pan. Transfer on to a plate, pour over the juices and leave to get cold. Cut the cold meat into very thin slices and remove any remaining fat before serving.

Serves 6–8

Steak Tartare

This is my idea of the slimmer's dream: a dozen oysters followed by steak tartare and a green salad. I could happily live on it but I don't because of the unfortunate fact that these are two of the most expensive dishes around.

Rump steak is best for the steak tartare as it has more flavour than the more tender fillet. It does have to be the best meat though, with every morsel of fat and gristle removed. The dish is high in protein but virtually devoid of calories.

1½ lb rump or fillet steak
½ teaspoon Worcestershire sauce
2 drops Tabasco sauce
½ teaspoon French Dijon mustard
½ tablespoon olive oil
½ tablespoon brandy
1 minced onion
Salt and pepper
4 eggs
2 tablespoons very finely-chopped parsley

Remove any fat and gristle from the meat and pass it twice through the coarse blades of a mincer. Mix together the Worcestershire sauce, Tabasco, mustard, olive oil and brandy. Add the meat and minced onion and mix well, season with salt and pepper. Shape the meat into four round cakes and make a well in the centre of each one. Break the eggs and slide one into the centre of each mound of meat, sprinkle with finely chopped parsley and serve.

The steak tartare should not be made too far in advance as the meat will lose its colour but it should be nicely cold. Ideally one should use meat which has been well chilled in the refrigerator and serve the dish as soon as it is made.

Cold Tongue with Sauce Vinaigrette

1 small fresh ox tongue
2 beef stock cubes
2 onions
2 carrots
4 sticks celery
Bouquet garni
8 peppercorns

The sauce

6 tablespoons olive oil
1 tablespoon white wine vinegar
½ teaspoon mustard
1 tablespoon capers
½ tablespoon finely-chopped gherkins
1 tablespoon finely-chopped chives
1 tablespoon finely-chopped parsley
Salt and freshly ground black pepper

Place the tongue in a saucepan with the stock cubes, the onions, peeled and roughly chopped, the carrots and celery, scraped and roughly chopped, the bouquet garni and peppercorns. Add enough water to cover, bring to the boil, cover and simmer for 2½–3 hours until tender. Cool for almost 1 hour in the stock, remove the tongue, strip off the skin and pull out any bones and return it to the stock to get quite cold. Carve into thin slices from the tip of the tongue and arrange in a serving dish. Combine all the ingredients for the sauce in a screw-top jar and shake well. Pour the sauce over the tongue and chill before serving.

Serves 6

Lamb Cutlets with Lemon Mint Jelly

For a fresh-tasting summer dish, there are few recipes to beat this one. The cutlets are marinated, grilled and then masked with a lemon mint jelly and the result is undeniably mouth-watering (not to mention being satisfyingly low on calories).

8 small lamb cutlets from the best end neck
2 tablespoons olive oil
1 tablespoon lemon juice
½ teaspoon rosemary
Salt and freshly ground black pepper
6 mint leaves
Juice 1 lemon
½ teaspoon gelatine
¼ pint water
1 bunch watercress

Trim off the fat from the cutlets and chine the ends (strip off the fat and meat from the top of the bone). Combine the olive oil and 1 tablespoon lemon juice with the rosemary, season with salt and pepper and brush the cutlets with this mixture. Leave them to marinate in a cold place for at least 2 hours.

Grill the cutlets under a high heat for about 4 minutes on each side until well-browned on the outside but still pink on the inside. Drain on kitchen paper and leave to cool.

Very finely chop the mint leaves, add them to the lemon juice and heat over a very low flame, to infuse the mint, for ten minutes. Add the gelatine, stir until the crystals have melted and mix in the water. Leave to cool. Arrange the cutlets in a shallow serving dish and when the jelly is beginning to set pour it over the cutlets making sure that the meat is evenly masked. Chill in a refrigerator until required and garnish with watercress.

Cold Brains with Yoghurt

A really sensational dish that is ideal to serve at a summer lunch party with a selection of other salads.

1 lb brains
¼ pint water
1 tablespoon vinegar
2 tablespoons olive oil
1 tablespoon white wine vinegar
½ teaspoon French Dijon mustard
Salt and freshly ground black pepper
1½ cartons yoghurt (7½ fl oz)
1 tablespoon tomato ketchup
2 oz firm button mushrooms
1 tablespoon grated raw onion
1 teaspoon finely-chopped dill
1 teaspoon paprika pepper

Wash the brains under cold running water and remove the veins and skin membrane. Combine the water and vinegar in a saucepan, add the brains, cover tightly and simmer gently for 15 minutes. Drain, press flat with a heavy plate and leave to cool. Cut the brains into thin matchstick strips. Combine the olive oil, white wine vinegar and mustard in a screw-top jar and shake to mix well. Season with salt and pepper, add the brains and leave to marinate for at least 1 hour. Drain off the marinade and mix in the yoghurt, tomato ketchup and paprika. Add the mushrooms, onion and dill and fold in the brains. Chill well before serving.

Salad of Calves' Brains

This makes an unusual and nutritious summer dish with a fresh light flavour.

1 lb calves' brains
¼ pint water
1 tablespoon vinegar
3 tablespoons olive oil
1 tablespoon white wine vinegar
1 teaspoon English mustard
Salt and freshly ground black pepper
4 tablespoons finely-chopped parsley
2 hard-boiled eggs
1 green or red pepper
2 sticks celery
2 tablespoons mayonnaise (see page 194)

Wash the brains under cold running water and remove all the veins and skin membrane. Combine the water and vinegar, bring to the boil and add the brains. Cover tightly and simmer gently for 20 minutes. Drain well, flatten with a heavy plate and leave to cool. Chop the brains into small dice. Combine the olive oil, white wine vinegar and mustard in a screw-top jar, season with salt and pepper, add the parsley and shake to mix well. Pour the dressing over the chopped brains and leave to marinate for at least 1 hour. Shell and chop the hard-boiled eggs. Remove the core and seeds of the pepper and finely chop the flesh. Thinly slice the celery. Add the egg, celery and green pepper to the brains and dressing, blend in the mayonnaise, mix lightly, check seasoning and chill before serving. Serve the salad on a bed of crisp lettuce leaves or surround with watercress.

Russian Chicken Salad

- ¾–1 lb cooked chicken
- 2 firm eating apples
- ½ lb cooked French beans
- 1 dill pickled cucumber
- 1 tablespoon pickled cucumber liquid
- ½ small white cabbage
- ¼ pint mayonnaise (see page 194)
- 1 teaspoon paprika pepper
- Salt

Cut the chicken into small dice. Peel, core and dice the apples. Cut the French beans into ¼ inch long pieces. Dice the pickled cucumber. Combine the chicken, apples, beans and cucumber. Blend the dill pickled cucumber liquid into the mayonnaise and season with salt and paprika. Finely shred the cabbage and arrange it round the edge of a serving dish. Pile the chicken salad in the centre and top with the dressing.

Special Chicken Salad

1 lb cooked chicken
3 celery stalks
6 stuffed olives
3 oz firm button mushrooms
¼ pint mayonnaise (see page 194)
1 carton sour cream (5 fl oz)
Salt and pepper
1 crisp lettuce

Cut the chicken into small dice. Remove the leaves of the celery and thinly slice the stalks. Chop 2 celery leaves and discard the rest. Thinly slice the stuffed olives and the mushrooms. Add the sour cream to the mayonnaise, folding it in and seasoning with salt and pepper. Fold in the chicken, olives, celery and mushrooms. Shred the lettuce and arrange it around a serving dish. Pile the chicken salad in the centre and chill before serving. Garnish with celery leaves.

Cold Chicken in Jellied Consommé

This is an attractive summer dish but it really does need the lift of fresh tarragon leaves. These are available in some of the better London delicatessens or charcuteries, but if you find it difficult to find the genuine article, tarragon can easily be grown in a pot in your kitchen window or in a window box. It is one of the nicest summer herbs. If the worst comes to the worst, use dried tarragon leaves but soak them for a good half hour in warm water flavoured with a little lemon juice to soften the herb and bring out the taste.

1 roasting chicken (about 3 lb)
2 tins consommé
1 pint water
Juice 1 lemon
1 tablespoon dry sherry
1 tablespoon (½ oz) gelatine
1 tablespoon fresh tarragon leaves

Place the chicken in a saucepan and pour over the consommé, water and lemon juice. Bring to the boil, cover and simmer gently for about 1½ hours until the chicken is tender. Remove the chicken from the liquid and leave to cool. Strain the consommé through a very fine sieve or muslin, remove any fat from the surface and add the sherry. Dissolve the gelatine in a little of the consommé and mix in the remaining liquid. Leave to cool and until the jelly begins to thicken.

Neatly carve the chicken into portions, remove all the skin and place them on a wire rack over a shallow dish. Decorate each joint with tarragon leaves and spoon over some consommé until the chicken is evenly coated. Continue to spoon over the jelly until a thick coating has formed. Arrange the joints on a serving dish and chill in a refrigerator. Chill any excess consommé and when set firm cut it into small cubes. Garnish the chicken joints with cubes of jellied consommé and sprigs of watercress.

Serve the chicken with a grapefruit and avocado salad.

Jellied Chicken and Bacon

1 onion
1 young boiling fowl
Bouquet garni
1 tablespoon sherry
2 lb bacon in a piece
2 cloves
1 tablespoon brown sugar
2 teaspoons white wine vinegar
Salt and pepper

Remove any coarse, earthy skins from the onion but leave on the inner brown skins and cut into quarters. Place the boiling fowl in a large pan with the onion and bouquet garni. Add sherry and just enough water to cover. Season with a little salt and pepper, bring to the boil and simmer slowly for about 1½ hours until the chicken is tender throughout.

Soak bacon if it has been salted, cover it with water, add the cloves, brown sugar and vinegar, bring slowly to the boil.

Skim off any scum from the surface, cover and simmer gently for 1½ – 2 hours until tender. Strain chicken liquid through a very fine sieve. Cut chicken and bacon into thin slices while still warm and pack tightly in a bowl in alternate layers. Remove all possible fat from the chicken stock (this can be done first with a spoon and then with absorbent kitchen paper). Pour enough stock into the bowl to cover the meat and top with a plate and a heavy weight. Cool and then leave to set in a refrigerator for at least 10 hours. Dip the mould into hot water, turn out and garnish with salad ingredients.

Vegetable dishes to go with anything – made without the fattening ingredients of melted butter and cream

VEGETABLES

Vegetables, especially fresh green varieties, are a boon to the person who wishes to keep slim. They provide nourishment and vitamins without loading on the calories and all at a very reasonable price.

In this book I have avoided the obvious temptations like potatoes. That is not to say that I feel potatoes should be completely debarred from a plan of sensible eating but merely that they are high in calorie content and therefore should be eaten in moderation. The least fattening way of serving potatoes (and also the most healthy) is to bake them in their jackets and serve them with sour cream and finely-chopped chives but as recipes for these and other potato dishes can be found in almost any basic cookery book I have omitted them here and used the space for more unusual ideas incorporating other vegetables.

There is a popular misconception that no vegetable is worth eating unless it is smothered generously with butter. Personally, I feel this is unnecessary; a spoonful of oil will do just the same job of lubrication and a touch of lemon juice with a seasoning of salt and freshly ground black pepper will give a much more exciting flavour.

All too often too little trouble and preparation is given to vegetables which are to be served as an accompaniment to a main dish. In many ways, they are just as important as the major recipe and two exciting vegetable dishes served with a plain main course can make the meal into something really special.

Vegetables should be served as fresh as possible. Never leave them sitting at room temperature for any length of time; never buy vegetables which have a dull and flabby appearance and avoid washing them more than is necessary. If vegetables do have to be kept for a day or two before cooking, wrap them in a polythene bag and store them in the bottom of a refrigerator or a really cold place like a cellar.

With vegetables that have to be peeled, cut the peel off as thinly as possible, as much of the goodness is contained towards the outer edge. Always avoid over-cooking or boiling in too much water as this will lead to a loss of flavour and goodness. The water which vegetables are cooked in, by the way, is well worth keeping to add to stock, soups or sauces.

ASPARAGUS

Asparagus is one of the delights of life and if you are like me you prefer to have it in large quantities occasionally than to be tantalized by a small quantity as a first course. I never believe in being stereotyped; if you like something then follow your own initiative and forget the rules and conventions. If asparagus is in season (whether it is the thin, green and well-flavoured stalks from our native soil or the fat, luscious fronds from across the sea) buy plenty, start the meal with a fairly substantial first course and have your asparagus as the main dish. Followed by cheese and fresh fruit, this makes one of the most perfect meals I know.

Serve the asparagus either hot or cold – it is equally good either way – but be careful not to overcook the stems; 15–20 minutes in boiling, salted water should be ample.

One of the classic accompaniments to asparagus is hot, melted butter but, since this is obviously an unfair temptation, serve instead a light vinaigrette with a basis of hard-boiled egg yolks. A little crisply fried and crumbled bacon can be added to the sauce to make it more substantial.

Sauce to Serve with Hot or Cold Asparagus

2 hard-boiled egg yolks
6 tablespoons olive oil
1 tablespoon white wine vinegar
1 tablespoon lemon juice
½ teaspoon finely-grated shallot or onion
Salt and freshly ground black pepper
1 rasher bacon, crisply-fried and crumbled

Mash the egg yolks with a fork until smooth. Season with salt and pepper and gradually beat in the olive oil with a wooden spoon, a drop at a time, to make an emulsion. When all the oil has been used up, blend in the vinegar and lemon juice, check the seasoning and add the onion and bacon.

French Beans with Hungarian Sauce

1 lb young green beans
4 oz firm button mushrooms
½ tablespoon olive oil
1 carton sour cream (5 fl oz)
1 teaspoon paprika pepper
Salt

Top and tail the beans. Thinly slice the mushrooms. Cook the beans in boiling, salted water for about 15 minutes until just tender. Heat the olive oil in a frying pan, add the mushrooms and cook over a medium high heat for 4 minutes. Drain off the excess oil. Combine the beans and mushrooms in a saucepan, add the sour cream, season with paprika and salt and heat through over a low flame without boiling.

Purée of Runner Beans

I am a fanatic about eating vegetables when they are young. The trouble about runner beans is that if you have to buy them from a greengrocer, they are inevitably thick and on the tough side. Puréeing the cooked beans solves this problem and the result is a satisfactory pale green colour which, if well seasoned, has a most agreeable taste.

1½ lb runner beans
Salt, pepper and a pinch cayenne pepper
1 egg yolk
4 tablespoons sour cream

Top and tail the beans, remove any coarse strings from the sides and cut them into thin slices. Cook the beans until tender in boiling, salted water, drain well and purée through a food mill, a sieve or in an electric liquidizer. Return the purée to a clean pan. Beat the egg yolk with sour cream. Blend the mixture into the purée of beans and season with salt, freshly ground black pepper and a pinch of cayenne. Heat through, stirring continually, but *do not allow to boil.*

Chinese Cabbage with Tomatoes

Chinese cabbage is a delicious vegetable and now fairly readily available in good greengrocers. The flesh is firm and the taste less strong than an English cabbage. Usually these cabbages grow very large and half a plant is enough for four servings.

½ Chinese cabbage
1 small onion
1 small tin tomatoes
Salt and freshly ground black pepper
¼ pint water

Cut the cabbage into ½-inch thick slices. Peel and finely chop the onion. Combine the cabbage with the water in a large saucepan. Season with salt and pepper, bring to the boil and simmer for 10 minutes. Add the onion and tomatoes and simmer for a further 6 – 10 minutes until the cabbage is just tender. Check seasoning before serving.

Special Creamed Cabbage

1 medium cabbage
1 oz butter
2 tablespoons sour cream
Salt and pepper
Small pinch nutmeg

Remove the outside leaves and core of the cabbage and finely shred the leaves. Cook in boiling, salted water for about six minutes until just tender and drain well. Purée the cabbage through a food mill or in an electric liquidizer and return to a clean pan. Add the butter and sour cream, mix well, season with salt, freshly ground black pepper and a pinch of nutmeg and heat through over a low heat.

Red Cabbage with Apple and Sour Cream

1 small red cabbage
1 onion
1 cooking apple
2 oz olive oil
2 tablespoons sour cream
Salt and pepper

Coarsely shred the cabbage. Peel and finely chop the onion. Peel and core the apple and cut into small dice. Heat the oil. Add the onion and cook over a medium heat until transparent. Mix in the cabbage, cover and cook for 15 minutes. Mix in the apple, cook for a further 5 minutes. Lower heat, mix in the sour cream, season with salt and pepper and heat through without boiling.

Baked Cabbage with Sour Cream

1 small head cabbage
1 clove garlic
1 small onion
1 oz bacon fat or butter
½ pint sour cream (10 fl oz)
Salt and pepper
1 teaspoon paprika pepper

Remove stem of cabbage and shred leaves. Press garlic clove through a garlic press. Peel and very finely chop onion. Melt bacon fat or butter. Add cabbage, garlic and onion and cook over a medium heat for three minutes. Season with salt, pepper and paprika and transfer to a baking dish. Pour over the sour cream and bake in a moderate oven (375°F, Reg 5) for 20 minutes.

Bulgarian Carrots

Like all root vegetables, carrots contain a certain amount of carbohydrates, but they are a useful and inexpensive vegetable and I would hate to do without those tender young ones which come early in the season. This recipe, which has a delicate flavour, looks appetizing and does without the traditional sugar and butter so often used in carrot dishes. The dish can be served hot or cold as a salad.

1 lb new carrots
Salt
2 cloves garlic
1 tablespoon finely-chopped parsley or chives
1 carton yoghurt (5 fl oz)
Freshly ground black pepper

Wash and scrub the carrots (avoid peeling if possible). Cut them into thin matchstick strips and cook in boiling, salted water until just tender but still slightly crisp – about 10 minutes. Drain well. Squeeze the garlic through a garlic press. Mix the garlic and parsley or chives into the yoghurt and season with salt and freshly ground black pepper.

To serve hot: Combine the yoghurt and carrots and heat through without boiling.

To serve cold: Pour the yoghurt over the carrots and chill in a refrigerator for at least an hour before serving.

Cauliflower with Yoghurt and Egg Sauce

1 cauliflower
1 tablespoon olive oil
2 teaspoons cornflour
1 carton yoghurt (5 fl oz)
2 hard-boiled eggs
Salt and pepper
Pinch of paprika

Cook the cauliflower in boiling, salted water until just tender. Drain well and keep warm.

Heat the olive oil in a saucepan, add the cornflour and cook over a medium heat, stirring continually until the mixture is smooth. Remove from the heat and blend in the yoghurt. Peel and chop the hard-boiled eggs. Add them to the sauce, season with salt, pepper and a pinch of paprika and heat through without boiling, stirring all the time. Pour the sauce over the cauliflower before serving.

Stock Boiled Celery with Cheese Topping

2 heads celery
½ pint stock
3 oz grated cheese
Paprika pepper

Remove the tough outside stalks of the celery. Remove any tough strings from the remaining stalks and trim off the leaves. Cut the celery into 5-inch-long strips about ½-inch wide.

Bring the stock to the boil, add the celery and simmer for 20 minutes or until tender. Transfer the celery to a shallow baking dish and pour over enough stock to come to a depth of ½ inch. Spread over the melted cheese, sprinkle with a generous seasoning of paprika and put under a hot grill until the cheese melts and becomes a rich golden brown.

Braised Celery Sticks

I love the taste of braised celery but hate the tough stringiness which is so often a feature of this dish. To ensure even cooking and tenderness, I cut the sticks into thin even strips before cooking them.

1 head celery
1 oz butter
½ pint stock
Salt and pepper

Divide celery and clean well. Trim off any stringy edges and cut sticks into 2-inch lengths about ¼-inch thick. Arrange them in a buttered fireproof dish (use half the butter) and pour over enough stock to cover. Dot with remaining butter, cover with tin foil and cook in a moderate oven (375°F, Reg 5) for 30–45 minutes until tender.

Courgettes in Tomato Sauce

1 lb courgettes
4 spring onions
4 tomatoes
1 clove garlic
¼ teaspoon coriander seeds
2 tablespoons olive oil
1 small bay leaf
Pinch paprika pepper
Salt
¼ pint cold water
1 tablespoon lemon juice

Top and tail the courgettes and cut the flesh into $\frac{1}{2}$-inch thick slices. Roughly chop the spring onions. Peel (see page xii) and chop the tomatoes. Peel and crush the garlic clove and lightly crush the coriander seeds. Heat the olive oil in a deep frying pan or saucepan, add the spring onions and garlic and cook for 2 minutes. Add the tomatoes, coriander, bay leaf, paprika, a pinch of salt and the cold water, bring to the boil and simmer gently for about 20 minutes until the courgettes are just tender but not mushy. Blend in the lemon juice and heat through.

This can also be served cold as a first course or salad.

LEEKS

Leeks are one of our most delicious winter vegetables, especially if they are picked when slim and slender. Their only problem is that of cleaning; mud and earth get down inside the layers of leaves and are difficult to extract. I find the best way to clean these roots is to cut off the coarse green tops, remove any outer leaves that are tough or discoloured and cut a nick with a sharp knife about a third of the way down the length. Wash the leeks under cold running water to flush out any dirt.

Cook leeks in boiling salted water until tender – 10–20 minutes depending on their size – and then drain them by standing the stalks upside down in a colander for a few minutes; in this way you should get rid of the moisture.

Serve plain boiled leeks with a spoonful of olive oil and a squeeze of lemon juice and season them with some freshly ground black pepper. Small leeks are delicious served as a first course or salad, well chilled and tossed in a vinaigrette dressing.

Arabian Leeks

6 medium leeks
3 tablespoons stock
2 tablespoons lemon juice
Salt and freshly ground black pepper
1 medium onion
1 clove garlic
2 oz black olives in brine
1 tablespoon olive oil
1 tin tomatoes (15 oz)
½ tablespoon finely-chopped parsley

Clean the leeks and arrange them in a fireproof baking dish. Pour over the stock and lemon juice and season with a little salt and pepper. Cover with foil and cook the leeks in a moderately hot oven (400°F, Reg 6) for about 20 minutes until just tender.

Peel and finely chop the onion. Crush the garlic clove. Halve the olives and remove the stones. Heat the olive oil in a saucepan, add the onion and garlic and cook over a medium heat until the onion is soft and transparent. Mix in the tomatoes and finely chopped parsley and continue to cook for a further 10 minutes. Season with salt and pepper and pour the sauce over the leeks. Top with the olives and return to a moderately hot oven for about five minutes to heat through.

MUSHROOMS

Mushrooms are about the most useful vegetable available for the slimmer. They add taste and flavouring to a great many dishes and are delicious as a vegetable in their own right, yet, remarkably, they contain absolutely no fattening components. Buy mushrooms that look white and firm and avoid washing them whenever possible. Do not overcook mushrooms when they are to be used as a vegetable as they lose their flavour and the pleasant texture.

Mushrooms with Sour Cream

½ lb firm button mushrooms
1 small onion
1 oz butter
1 carton sour cream (5 fl oz)
Salt and freshly ground black pepper

Slice the mushrooms. Peel and finely chop the onion. Heat the butter in a saucepan, add the onion and cook over a medium heat, without browning, until the onion is soft and transparent. Add the mushrooms and cook for a further 3 minutes. Mix in the sour cream, season with salt and pepper and heat through without boiling.

Savoury Stuffed Onions

8 medium onions
3 rashers lean bacon
1 oz butter
4 tomatoes
Salt and freshly ground black pepper
¼ pint stock

Peel the onions and cut a thin slice off the bottom so that they stand upright. Using a sharp knife, cut out the centre of the onions to within ¼ inch of the bottom. Finely chop the onion which has been removed. Mince the bacon and peel and finely chop the tomatoes. Melt the butter in a saucepan, add the chopped onion and bacon and cook over a medium heat for 4 minutes. Mix in the tomatoes, season with salt and pepper and continue to simmer for about 5 minutes. Fill the centre of the onions with the tomato mixture and place them in a baking dish with the stock. Bake the onions in a very moderate oven (350°F, Reg 4) for 40 minutes or until tender.

Pepperato

A delicious mixture of peppers, tomatoes and onion which goes well with almost any main dish. It can be served hot or cold.

3 green or red peppers
1 large onion
1 lb tomatoes
2 tablespoons olive oil
4 anchovy fillets
Freshly ground black pepper

Remove the core and seeds of the peppers and cut the flesh into thin rings. Peel and very thinly slice the onion and divide into rings. Peel the tomatoes (see page xii), remove the seeds and cut the flesh into small dice. Finely chop the anchovy fillets. Heat the olive oil in a heavy saucepan. Add the peppers and onion and cook over a medium heat for about five minutes until the onions are transparent. Add the tomatoes and anchovy fillets and season with freshly ground black pepper. Cover tightly and simmer for 30 minutes.

Salsify with Tomatoes

Salsify is justifiably known as the oyster plant. Its texture and flavour is so delicate that it does indeed remind one of those delicious riches of the sea. Salsify is a difficult plant to deal with because it needs careful peeling or scraping and must then be plunged immediately into cold water with the juice of ½ lemon incorporated into it, or the delicate root will brown and discolour.

A slight cheat (but a far less troublesome way to produce this delicious vegetable) is to buy tinned salsify from a delicatessen. The calorie content may be a little higher through the process of canning but nevertheless time, for most of us, is at a premium.

1 medium tin tomatoes
Salt and freshly ground black pepper
Pinch cayenne pepper
8 salsify roots (or 1 tin salsify)

Heat the tomatoes in a saucepan, season with salt, pepper and a little cayenne and mix well. Peel or scrape the salsify roots, cut into matchstick lengths 2-inches long by ½ inch thick and drop immediately into cold water combined with the juice of half a lemon. When all the salsify has been prepared, add it to the tomatoes, cover tightly and simmer for 15–20 minutes until tender.

Spinach with Onion Flakes

1 lb leaf spinach
2 tablespoons finely-chopped onion
1 tablespoon olive oil
Juice ½ lemon
Salt and freshly ground black pepper

Wash the spinach and remove any tough stalks. Shake well and put the spinach in a saucepan without any additional water. Season with a little salt and simmer gently for 10 minutes until just tender. Spread the chopped onion on a lightly-oiled baking sheet and bake in a moderate oven (375°F, Reg 5) for 5 – 8 minutes until crisp and golden brown. Pour the olive oil and lemon juice over the spinach, season with salt and freshly ground black pepper and toss lightly. Arrange the spinach in a serving dish and top with the browned onion flakes.

Stuffed Baked Tomatoes

8 medium large ripe tomatoes
½ lb broccoli tops
½ oz melted butter
Salt and freshly ground black pepper
2 oz grated cheddar cheese

Peel the tomatoes (see page xii), cut a slice off the top and scoop out the centre, leaving about a ¼ inch thickness of shell. Remove the seeds and finely chop the flesh.

Cook the broccoli in boiling, salted water until tender. Drain well and mix with the melted butter and tomato pulp. Season with salt and freshly ground black pepper and fill the tomato shells with the mixture. Top with grated cheese and bake in a very moderate oven (350°F, Reg 4) for 20 minutes until golden brown.

Tomatoes Baked with Cheese

½ lb firm tomatoes
1 onion
1 green pepper
2 tablespoons olive oil
Salt and pepper
1 oz grated cheddar cheese
½ oz grated parmesan cheese

Thinly slice the tomatoes and arrange them in a lightly oiled fireproof serving dish. Peel and finely chop the onion. Remove the core and seeds of the pepper and finely chop the flesh. Heat 1 tablespoon of olive oil in a saucepan, add the onion and pepper and cook over a low heat for 5 minutes until they are soft.

Spread the onion and pepper over the tomatoes and season with salt and pepper. Top with the mixed cheddar and parmesan cheese and dribble over the remaining oil. Bake in a very moderate oven (350°F, Reg 4) until the cheese has melted and the top is golden brown (about 15 – 20 minutes).

Grilled Tomatoes with Lemon Juice and Herbs

This has a rather sharp taste which goes well with all meat dishes. It is especially good if one can find fresh oregano.

6 medium tomatoes
1 tablespoon olive oil
1 tablespoon lemon juice
1 teaspoon oregano
Salt and freshly ground black pepper

Halve the tomatoes and arrange them cut side up in a shallow baking dish or on the grill pan. Combine the olive oil, lemon juice, oregano and seasoning. Brush the surface of the tomatoes with this mixture and grill them under a medium high heat for about five minutes until the tops are lightly scorched.

RICE

Although rice is basically very starchy, it is also filling and makes a satisfactory accompaniment to many main courses. If the rice is well rinsed to remove excess starch during the cooking process, it can make a useful and versatile side dish.

Slim Jim Rice

Extra flavour is added in this recipe with a little olive oil and a seasoning of salt and freshly ground black pepper.

8 oz long grain or Patna rice
3½ pints water
1 tablespoon olive oil
Salt and pepper

Place the rice in a colander or sieve and rinse it with cold running water. Bring 2 pints water to the boil, add the rice and cook over a high heat for 5 minutes. Drain off the water, rinse the rice again in cold running water and return it to a second pan of 1½ pints boiling water. Bring back to the boil and cook for a further 10 minutes or until the rice is just tender (it should not be soft and soggy). Rinse the rice once more in first cold and then warm water, drain it well and return to a clean pan over a low heat to dry out the excess moisture. Add the olive oil, season with salt and freshly ground black pepper and mix well. Turn on to a heated serving dish.

Variations:

Mushroom Rice

8 oz rice cooked as above
2 oz firm button mushrooms
1 tablespoon olive oil
Salt and freshly ground black pepper
½ teaspoon lemon juice

Cook the rice and leave it in a clean pan over a low heat for a few minutes to remove extra moisture. Very thinly slice the mushrooms. Heat the olive oil in a frying pan, add the mushrooms and cook over a medium heat for three minutes. Lightly mix the mushrooms and juices to the rice and season with salt and freshly ground black pepper and lemon juice and turn on to a heated serving dish.

Herby Rice

8 oz rice, cooked as above
1 teaspoon dried mixed herbs
4 tablespoons stock
1 tablespoon finely-chopped parsley

Add the dried herbs to the stock and simmer gently over a very low heat for 5 minutes to bring out the flavour. Cook the rice and leave it in a clean pan over a low heat for a few minutes to remove extra moisture. Mix in the stock, herbs and finely-chopped parsley and turn on to a heated serving dish.

Rice with Red and Green Peppers

8 oz rice, cooked as above
½ red and ½ green pepper
½ tablespoon olive oil
Salt and pepper

Remove the core and seeds of the peppers and finely chop the flesh. Cook the peppers in boiling salted water for five minutes and drain well. Cook the rice and leave it in a clean saucepan over a low heat for a few minutes to remove extra moisture. Add the peppers and olive oil, season with salt and pepper, mix well and turn on to a heated serving dish.

Chinese Style Rice

8 oz rice cooked as above
4 thin rashers lean bacon
1 egg
Pepper

Cook the rice and leave it in a clean saucepan over a low heat for a few minutes to remove extra moisture. Cut off the rinds of the bacon and finely chop the rashers. Fry the rind and chopped bacon over a medium high heat for three minutes and discard the rinds. Add the bacon and bacon fat to the rice and mix well. Beat the egg and mix it into the hot rice, stirring until the egg just begins to set. Season with pepper and turn on to a heated serving dish.

Salads to serve at any time and on any occasion

SALADS

Salads are synonymous with slimming; they look attractive and help to provide a well-balanced diet as they supply vitamin C and a good proportion of mineral salts. Fairly plain salads can be served in place of a vegetable with a main course and there is a wide range of more substantial salad dishes which make the basis of a meal in their own right.

Salad ingredients should be fresh and crisp. If the ingredients need to be washed they should be rinsed under icy cold water, never left to soak, and should be shaken dry to get rid of as much water as possible and then lightly dabbed with a clean tea cloth or kitchen paper. Salad ingredients which are to be kept for a day or two should be washed if necessary, dried well and stored in polythene bags in the bottom of the refrigerator or in a really cold place like a cellar.

Even a plain salad will benefit from a little garnishing; some finely-chopped chives or fresh herbs, for instance, or a little finely-chopped red pepper.

SOME ADVICE ABOUT PREPARING SALADS

The Chinese are masters in the art of making food look attractive and their salads are a dream of artistry. Their secret lies in the chopping and slicing of the raw ingredients and is a practice well worth trying to emulate. Use a really sharp knife and if the ingredients are to be sliced, cut as near wafer thin as possible. If the ingredients are to be chopped or diced try to keep the pieces uniform in size.

Cucumber is a popular salad ingredient but it does contain a high percentage of water and can make other ingredients soggy, especially if the salad is served with a mayonnaise or dressing. Avoid this by slicing the cucumber really thinly, sprinkling the slices with a little salt and spreading them out on a flat plate. Leave the slices to 'sweat' for about an hour and then drain them well and pat dry on kitchen paper before using.

If tomatoes are to be used in a salad, unless they are of the large continental variety, they benefit from being skinned; do this by dropping the tomatoes into boiling water for 30 seconds and then sliding off the skins which should be easily detached.

Watercress is another useful and attractive ingredient to use in salads and as a garnish but it does go limp very easily. Remove the rubber bands or string from bunches of watercress as soon as possible, snip off the bottom of the stalks and stand them in a container of cold water. In this way, the watercress should keep fresh for at least two or three days.

Pepper, Onion and Olive Salad

When possible, buy loose olives from a delicatessen as these tend to be far less salty than the tinned or bottled varieties.

- 2 peppers (red if possible but green will do)
- 1 onion
- ¼ lb black olives
- 3 tablespoons olive oil
- 1 tablespoon white wine vinegar
- Salt and freshly ground black pepper
- ½ teaspoon French Dijon mustard

Remove the outer skins of the peppers by holding them over an open flame until the skin cracks, as it will then peel off easily or by baking in a hot oven for about 15 minutes. Leave to cool, peel off the skins, cut off the stems and remove the core and seeds from the centres. Cut the peppers into the thinnest possible rings. Peel the onion, cut into very thin slices and then separate into rings. Cut the olives into thin slivers and discard the stones. Arrange the peppers, onion and olives in a serving dish. Combine the olive oil, vinegar, mustard and seasoning in a screw-top jar and shake well until all the ingredients are well blended. Pour the dressing over the salad, toss lightly and chill in a refrigerator for at least half an hour before serving.

Cold Mushrooms with Sour Cream

Mushrooms have the attraction of being full of flavour without being in the least fattening. Served as a salad without being cooked, they make a delicious summer vegetable.

4 oz firm button mushrooms
2 spring onions
1 carton sour cream (5 fl oz)
Salt and pepper
Pinch paprika pepper

Cut mushrooms into paper-thin slices. Finely chop onions. Season the sour cream with salt and pepper and fold in the mushrooms and onions. Arrange on a serving dish and sprinkle the top with a little paprika pepper. Chill before serving.

French Bean Salad with Bacon

Cooked stringless green beans make the most delicious salad, fresh and crisp, and I never can understand why they are not served this way more often in this country. Rinse the beans in cold water as soon as they are tender to crisp the flesh and prevent the beans from over-cooking.

1½ lb French beans
2 rashers lean bacon
1 small clove garlic
3 tablespoons olive oil
1 tablespoon white wine vinegar
½ teaspoon French Dijon mustard
Salt and freshly ground black pepper

Top and tail the beans and cook them in boiling salted water for about 8 minutes until just tender (this depends on the size, and the thinner they are the more delicious they taste). Drain them well and rinse at once under cold running water.

Cook the bacon rashers without any extra fat in a frying pan over a medium high heat until crisp, drain well on kitchen paper to remove excess fat, leave to cool, cut off the rinds and crumble the rashers into small pieces. Crush the garlic clove. Combine the olive oil, vinegar, mustard, garlic and seasoning in a screw-top jar and shake well. Pour the dressing over the beans and toss lightly. Turn on to a serving dish, top with the crumbled bacon and chill before serving.

Salad of Mange-Tout Peas, and Carrots

As a vegetable salad, this is hard to beat. The peas and carrots should be cooked until just tender, but still crisp, and then tossed while hot in a herb French dressing. Chill the dish before serving.

½ lb mange-tout peas
2 carrots
3 tablespoons olive oil
1 tablespoon white wine vinegar
1 teaspoon dry English mustard
Salt and freshly ground black pepper
½ tablespoon finely-chopped parsley
¼ teaspoon basil (or 3 fresh basil leaves)
Pinch tarragon

Top and tail the pea pods and leave whole. Peel the carrots and cut them into thin matchstick lengths about 2 inches long and ¼ inch thick. Drop the carrots into boiling, salted water and cook for 15 minutes. Add the pea pods and continue to cook for a further 10 minutes until the vegetables are just tender but still crisp. Drain well.

Combine the olive oil, mustard and vinegar in a screw-top

jar, season with salt and pepper and add the herbs. Shake to mix well and pour the dressing over the hot vegetables. Cool and then chill in a refrigerator for at least two hours before serving.

A Salad to Serve with Roast Duck or Wild Duck

2 red or green peppers
1 large orange
1 large onion
2 mint leaves
3 tablespoons olive oil
1 tablespoon white wine vinegar
Salt and freshly ground black pepper

Remove the core and seeds from the peppers and cut the flesh into thin rings. Peel the orange, remove any white pith or membrane and cut the flesh into thin slices, removing any pips. Peel the onion, slice very thinly and divide into rings. Finely chop the mint. Combine the olive oil and vinegar in a screw-top jar, season with salt and pepper, and shake well. Combine the peppers, orange slices and onion in a serving dish, pour over the dressing, sprinkle over the mint leaves and chill well before serving.

Broccoli Salad

1½ lb purple or green sprouting broccoli spears (or 2 packets frozen broccoli)
¼ pint vinaigrette dressing (see page 191)

Trim fresh broccoli and cook in boiling water until just tender (about 20 minutes), drain well (reserving the liquid for use as stock) and leave to cool. Toss the broccoli in vinaigrette dressing and serve well chilled.

Courgettes and Bacon Salad

It wasn't until I grew my own courgettes and found they flourished so well I was up to my ears in the things that I discovered how delicious the young vegetables are eaten raw as a salad. Choose very small, firm and crisp courgettes with no blemishes.

1 lb baby courgettes
3 tablespoons olive oil
1 tablespoon white wine vinegar
½ teaspoon French Dijon mustard
2 teaspoons chopped chives or spring onion tops
Salt and freshly ground black pepper
4 thin rashers lean bacon

Wash the courgettes and dry well but do not peel. Cut them into ¼ inch thick slices and put into a serving dish. Combine the olive oil, vinegar, mustard, chives and seasoning in a screw-top jar and shake well. Pour the dressing over the courgettes. Fry the bacon over a medium high heat, without extra fat, until crisp. Drain well on kitchen paper and leave to cool. Crumble the bacon and sprinkle it over the courgettes.

Marinated Celery

2 heads celery
1 clove garlic
3 tablespoons olive oil
1 tablespoon white wine vinegar
1 teaspoon French Dijon mustard
¼ teaspoon tarragon
Salt and freshly ground black pepper

Remove the tough outer stalks of the celery. Remove any tough strings from the inner stalks and trim off the tops. Cut the stalks into thin matchstick strips about 5 inches long and ¼ inch thick. Steam the stalks in a colander over boiling water for about 20–30 minutes until tender but still crisp. Leave to cool. Squeeze the garlic through a garlic press. Combine the garlic, olive oil, vinegar, mustard and tarragon, seasoned with salt and freshly ground black pepper in a screw-top jar and shake to mix well. Pour the dressing over the celery and chill for at least two hours in a refrigerator.

Serve as one dish of assorted hors d'oeuvres or as a salad.

Friday's Child's Salad

1 small swede
3 carrots
4 sticks celery
1 tablespoon finely-chopped gherkins
½ pint mayonnaise
1 teaspoon mustard

Peel the swede and cut the flesh into thin matchstick strips. Blanch the strips in boiling salted water for 2 minutes. Drain well and cool. Peel carrots and cut into thin matchstick strips. Thinly slice celery stalks. Combine gherkins, mayonnaise and mustard and mix well. Check seasoning and mix in vegetables. Chill the salad before serving.

Raw Carrot Salad

Being made from a root vegetable, this is quite high in calories and this should be balanced by the ingredients in the main course which it accompanies.

1 lb firm, crisp carrots
2 tablespoons olive oil
2 teaspoons white wine vinegar
3 tablespoons sour cream
Salt and freshly ground black pepper

Peel the carrots and grate them through the coarse blades of a grater or shred through a food mill. Beat the olive oil and vinegar into the sour cream, season with salt and pepper and mix in the finely chopped chives. Fold in the grated carrots and chill before serving.

Mushroom and Green Pepper Salad

¼ lb firm button mushrooms
2 green peppers
1 carton yoghurt (5 fl oz)
1 tablespoon tomato ketchup
1 teaspoon lemon juice
1 tablespoon finely-chopped chives or spring onion tops
Salt
Pinch paprika pepper

Thinly slice the mushrooms. Remove the core and seeds of the green peppers and cut the flesh into thin strips. Mix the yoghurt with the tomato ketchup and lemon juice, and season with salt and a little paprika. Pour the dressing over the vegetables, toss lightly and chill before serving.

Spinach Salad

Raw Spinach Salad

Raw spinach is delicious and makes a good substitute for lettuce in the winter months.

½ lb spinach
2 oz firm button mushrooms
3 tablespoons olive oil
1 tablespoon lemon juice
½ teaspoon French Dijon mustard
1 teaspoon grated onion
Salt and freshly ground black pepper

Wash the spinach in plenty of cold, salted water, trim off the stalks and shake well to dry thoroughly. Roughly shred the leaves and place them in a serving bowl. Very thinly slice the mushrooms and add them to the spinach. Combine the olive oil, lemon juice, mustard and grated onion, season with salt and pepper and mix well. Pour the dressing over the salad, toss lightly and chill in a refrigerator until required.

Cooked Spinach Salad

1 lb spinach
4 tablespoons olive oil
1 tablespoon lemon juice
Salt and pepper
Pinch nutmeg
2 rashers lean bacon

Wash the spinach and discard any tough stalks. Place the spinach in a saucepan without any extra water, add a little salt, cover and simmer gently for 10 minutes until the spinach is just tender. Drain off any excess liquid, add the olive oil and lemon juice and season with salt and pepper. Toss lightly and leave to get cold.

Remove the bacon rinds and fry the rashers without any extra fat until crisp. Drain on kitchen paper, crumble into small pieces and sprinkle the bacon over the salad.

Italian Tomato Salad

If you grow your own herbs, fresh basil in the summer makes all the difference to anything made with tomatoes, imparting a delicious, fresh taste. Fresh basil can also be bought from some of the better food stores.

Mozzarella cheese is now available from most good delicatessen shops and is essential to this salad, which is served as a first course in many areas of Italy.

- 4 large firm ripe tomatoes
- 2 oz mozzarella cheese
- 1 tablespoon finely-chopped chives
- 4 anchovy fillets
- 1 small clove garlic
- 3 tablespoons olive oil
- 1 tablespoon white wine vinegar
- Salt and freshly ground black pepper

Using a very sharp knife, thinly slice the tomatoes and arrange them in a glass serving dish. Thinly slice the cheese and place the slices on top of the tomatoes. Sprinkle over the chopped chives. Cut the anchovy fillets into very thin strips and arrange them in a lattice pattern on top of the salad. Crush the garlic and combine it in a screw-top jar with the olive oil, vinegar and seasoning. Shake well and pour the dressing over the salad.

Aylesbury Tomato Salad

- 4 large firm tomatoes
- 3 stalks celery
- 1 small onion
- 3 tablespoons olive oil
- 1 tablespoon white wine vinegar
- 1 teaspoon French Dijon mustard
- $\frac{1}{4}$ teaspoon tarragon
- Salt and pepper

Peel the tomatoes (see page 175) and cut them into thin slices. Trim off the celery leaves and any tough fibres and cut the stalks into thin slices. Peel and very thinly slice the onion and divide into rings. Combine the salad ingredients in a serving dish. Combine the olive oil, vinegar, mustard and seasoning in a screw-top jar with the tarragon. Shake well and pour the dressing over the salad. Chill before serving.

Grapefruit and Avocado Salad

The sharp taste of grapefruit makes a good contrast to the rather smooth, creamy texture of avocados. This is a salad which can be served as a first course and which goes well as an accompaniment to plain poultry or fish main courses.

Tinned grapefruit can be used instead of fresh fruit but there is the disadvantage that tinned fruit is usually packed in a heavy sugar syrup.

2 grapefruit
2 avocados
2 tablespoons olive oil
1 tablespoon lemon juice
Salt and freshly ground black pepper
2 oz black olives in brine

Peel the grapefruit and divide into segments. Remove the white pith and skin from each segment and take out any pips. Arrange the grapefruit in a shallow serving dish. Peel the avocados, cut each one into half and remove the stone. Cut the flesh into $\frac{1}{4}$-inch thick slices and add them to the grapefruit. Combine the olive oil and lemon juice, season with salt and pepper and mix well. Pour the dressing over the grapefruit and avocados and top with the black olives cut into thin strips. Chill in a refrigerator before serving.

Watercress and Grapefruit Salad

1 small tin grapefruit segments
2 bunches watercress
2 tablespoons olive oil
1 teaspoon French Dijon mustard
1 tablespoon white wine vinegar
Salt and freshly ground black pepper

Drain off all the juice from the grapefruit segments. Cut off the tough stalks from the watercress and combine with the grapefruit in a serving dish. Combine the olive oil, mustard and vinegar in a screw-top jar, season with salt and pepper and shake to mix well. Pour the dressing over the watercress and grapefruit and toss lightly.

Watercress, Orange and Chicory Salad

1 bunch watercress
2 heads chicory
2 large oranges
4 tablespoons olive oil
1 tablespoon white wine vinegar
Salt and freshly ground black pepper

Wash the watercress, trim off the tough ends of the stalks and shake well to dry. Trim the outer leaves and ends of the chicory and cut into thin slices. Peel the oranges, remove any pith and white membrane and cut into thin slices (removing any pips). Combine the salad ingredients in a serving dish. Combine the oil and vinegar, season with salt and pepper and mix well, pour over the salad ingredients and toss lightly. Chill before serving.

Franques Salad

½ lb cooked beetroot
4 stalks celery
½ lb cooking apples
1 dill pickled cucumber
1 medium onion
3 tablespoons white wine vinegar
2 tablespoons olive oil
2 tablespoons sour cream
Salt and pepper

Cut the beetroot into small dice. Thinly slice the celery. Peel and core the apples and cut into small dice. Dice the pickled cucumber and finely chop the onion. Combine the vinegar, olive oil and sour cream in a screw-top jar, season with salt and pepper and shake until well blended. Pour the dressing over the salad ingredients, mix well and chill for at least 30 minutes before serving.

Cauliflower with Black Olives and Green Peppers

1 small cauliflower
8 black olives
1 green pepper
1 teaspoon French Dijon mustard
1 egg yolk
¼ pint olive oil
1 tablespoon white wine vinegar
2 tablespoons yoghurt
Salt and pepper

Remove outer leaves of the cauliflower, separate the florettes and cook them in boiling salted water until tender but still crunchy. Drain well and cool. Remove stones from the black olives and cut the flesh into thin strips. Remove core and seeds of the green pepper and finely chop the flesh. Beat mustard and egg yolk together for at least two minutes. Gradually add the olive oil, beating continually and adding the oil only drop by drop until the sauce is thick and all the oil has been absorbed. Slowly beat in the vinegar and season with salt and pepper.

Arrange the cauliflower on a serving dish and spoon over the sauce. Sprinkle the olives and green pepper over the surface and serve chilled.

Cucumber Salad

One of the most refreshing of summer salads.

1 cucumber
Salt and freshly ground black pepper
2 tablespoons finely-chopped chives
1 tablespoon olive oil
3 tablespoons white wine vinegar

Peel and very thinly slice the cucumber. Arrange slices in a shallow serving dish and sprinkle over the chopped chives. Combine olive oil and vinegar, season with salt and pepper and mix well. Pour the dressing over the cucumber and chill in a refrigerator for at least an hour before serving.

Cucumber and Black Olive Salad

Served with cold chicken or ham, this salad helps to turn a rather mundane meal into something special.

1 medium cucumber
12 black olives
1 carton sour cream (5 fl oz)
Salt and pepper
Pinch paprika pepper
Juice ½ lemon
1 teaspoon French Dijon mustard
1 tablespoon finely-chopped chives

Peel and thinly slice cucumber. Remove stones from the olives and cut the flesh into thin slivers. Mix sour cream with lemon juice and mustard and season with salt, pepper and a pinch of paprika.

Fold cucumber and olives into the sour-cream dressing and place in a shallow serving dish. Chill well and sprinkle the chives over the surface before serving.

Cabbage and Bacon Salad

When lettuces are expensive or those available are only the frankly floppy variety, crisp white cabbage makes a good alternative. In this recipe the cabbage/bacon combination results in an interesting pleasant side dish which goes well with almost any main course.

½ firm white cabbage
2½ tablespoons white wine vinegar
1 tablespoon olive oil
1 teaspoon caraway seeds
Salt and pepper
Pinch caster sugar
4 rashers lean bacon

Remove core and finely shred cabbage. Combine vinegar, olive oil, sugar, seasoning and caraway seeds and mix well. Toss shredded cabbage in the dressing. Fry bacon without any extra fat until crisp. Drain on kitchen paper and leave to cool. Crumble the bacon into small pieces. Arrange cabbage in a serving dish and sprinkle over the bacon just before serving.

A few sauces to add a sparkle to some of the more simple dishes

What is sauce for the goose may be sauce for the gander but it also may not be a sauce for the weightwatcher. Take an Hollandaise, for instance – a most delicious concoction but one that can't be made with less than about 6 oz of butter and think what that does to one's waistline. It always amuses me that so many weight-conscious Americans really do seem convinced that an Oeuf Benedictine is a slimmer's dish. I have seen them happily tuck into a bread roll or muffin, topped by a thick piece of ham and a poached egg, all generously coated in Hollandaise, and smugly applaud their self-control – then they wonder sadly why the scales keep rising!

Unfortunately, many sauces, especially those found in the more expensive restaurants, are fattening. They tend to have butter and flour bases and more often than not they have a liberal addition of thick cream to give them that smooth and shiny appearance. Avoid these if you can; thicken with egg yolks rather than a liberal amount of flour or cream and make good use of non-fattening ingredients such as tomatoes, home-made stock, onions and mushrooms in your sauces.

Vinaigrette Dressings

Most salads need a dressing of some kind or another and, although a classical vinaigrette is made up of three parts olive oil to 1 part vinegar or lemon juice, the acidity of the vinegar or lemon juice counteracts the oil. Vinaigrette dressings are most commonly used on cold ingredients but I also find them delicious for hot vegetables. Young beans, for instance, carrots, spinach and other green vegetables will benefit from a vinaigrette rather than a more traditional dressing of melted butter.

Plain Vinaigrette Dressing or French Dressing

3 tablespoons olive oil
1 tablespoon white wine vinegar or lemon juice
½ teaspoon French Dijon mustard
Salt and freshly ground black pepper

Combine all the ingredients in a screw-top jar, season with salt and freshly ground black pepper and shake to mix well.

For a garlic dressing, add a peeled clove of garlic to the dressing and leave for at least 30 minutes before using. Remove the garlic before pouring the dressing over the salad or vegetables.

Tomato French Dressing

1 tomato
3 tablespoons olive oil
1 tablespoon white wine vinegar
½ teaspoon French Dijon mustard
Salt and freshly ground black pepper

Peel the tomato (see page 175), remove the seeds and finely chop the flesh. Combine all the ingredients in a screw-top jar and shake to mix well.

Herb Vinaigrette

3 tablespoons olive oil
1 tablespoon white wine vinegar
½ teaspoon French Dijon mustard
Salt and freshly ground black pepper
1 tablespoon finely-chopped chives
1 teaspoon chervil
Pinch tarragon
Pinch marjoram

Combine all the ingredients in a screw-top jar and shake to mix well. Leave to stand for 20 minutes and shake again before using. Use with salads or hot vegetables.

Onion Dressing

3 tablespoons olive oil
1 tablespoon white wine vinegar
½ teaspoon French Dijon mustard
Salt and freshly ground black pepper
1 onion or 1 small shallot or 3 spring onions

Coarsely grate the shallot or onion or very thinly slice the spring onions. Combine all the ingredients in a screw-top jar, season with salt and freshly ground black pepper, and shake to mix well.

Caper and Olive Dressing

1 teaspoon capers
6 stuffed olives
3 tablespoons olive oil
½ tablespoon lemon juice
½ teaspoon French Dijon mustard
Freshly ground black pepper

Finely chop the capers. Thinly slice the stuffed olives. Combine the olive oil, lemon juice, mustard and capers in a screw-top jar and season with freshly ground black pepper. Shake to mix well, add the olives and serve with vegetable or fish salads.

French Dressing with Hard-boiled eggs

1 hard-boiled egg
½ teaspoon French Dijon mustard
3 tablespoons olive oil
1 tablespoon white wine vinegar
Salt and freshly ground black pepper

Shell the egg and separate the white from the yolk. Mash the yolk with the mustard until smooth. Gradually blend in the olive oil, a little at a time, and then blend in the vinegar. Season with salt and pepper. Very finely chop the hard-boiled egg white and add it to the dressing.

This is delicious with cold artichokes, asparagus and other green vegetables.

Other Salad and Vegetable Dressings

Sour Cream Dressing

½ teaspoon French Dijon mustard
3 tablespoons lemon juice
1 carton sour cream (5 fl oz)
1 clove garlic or ½ tablespoon finely-grated onion
Salt and freshly ground black pepper
Pinch paprika pepper

Combine the mustard and lemon juice and mix until smooth. Add this mixture to the sour cream and mix well. Season with salt, freshly ground black pepper and a pinch paprika and stir in the garlic, pressed through a garlic press, or the onion just before serving.

A good dressing for bean salads, fish or shellfish.

Yoghurt and Pepper Dressing

1 carton yoghurt (5 fl oz)
1 tablespoon tomato ketchup
1 tablespoon lemon juice
1 tablespoon finely-chopped green or red pepper
Salt
Pinch paprika pepper

Combine the yoghurt, tomato ketchup and lemon juice and mix well. Add the chopped pepper and season with salt and paprika.

Yoghurt and Prawn Dressing

1 carton yoghurt (5 fl oz)
2 tablespoons lemon juice
Few drops Tabasco sauce
Pinch salt
2 oz peeled prawns
1 tablespoon finely-grated onion

Combine the yoghurt and lemon juice and season with a few drops of Tabasco and a little salt. Finely chop the prawns and add them to the dressing with the grated onion. Mix well and chill before serving.

Mayonnaise

Basic Mayonnaise

This makes ½ pint mayonnaise.

2 egg yolks
½ teaspoon dry English mustard
Salt and pepper
½ pint olive oil
1½ tablespoons vinegar or lemon juice

Combine the egg yolks and mustard, season with a little salt and pepper and beat well. Beating all the time, add the olive oil a few drops at a time. Do not add more olive oil until the previous addition has been completely absorbed by the egg yolks and has become emulsified. When all the oil has been used up, beat in the vinegar or lemon juice. Check seasoning before serving.

Slimmers' Mayonnaise

¼ pint mayonnaise

1 carton yoghurt or sour cream (5 fl oz)

Combine the mayonnaise and yoghurt or sour cream and mix well. Check seasoning before serving.

Hawkin's Mayonnaise

A somewhat sharp-flavoured sauce which gives an exciting flavour to cold roast beef or cold ham.

½ pint mayonnaise
1 tablespoon French Dijon mustard
1 tablespoon made horseradish sauce
1 teaspoon freshly-grated raw onion

Add the Dijon mustard to the mayonnaise and mix well. Fold in the horseradish sauce and grated onion, pile into a bowl and chill in a refrigerator until required.

Johnson's Mayonnaise for Cold Roast Beef

Juicy rare thin slices of cold roast beef make a delicious summer luncheon dish. Instead of serving the meat with the conventional accompaniments of horseradish sauce and mustard, combine them both with mayonnaise in this unusual sauce.

- ½ pint home-made mayonnaise
- 1 tablespoon French Dijon mustard
- 1 pickled gherkin
- 6 black olives
- 1 tablespoon horseradish sauce
- Salt and pepper

Very finely chop the gherkin and the flesh of the black olives. Combine all the ingredients, mix well and season with salt and pepper. Double quantities of the sauce can be made and any residue stored in the refrigerator in a screw-topped jar or tightly-lidded polythene container.

Other Sauces and Dressings

Fresh Tomato Sauce

If you own a deep freeze, make plenty of this sauce when tomatoes are at their cheapest and stock up for the winter. It keeps well and can be used in any number of dishes. If the dish is to be frozen, omit the garlic and add it when reheating.

- ½ lb ripe tomatoes
- 1 large onion
- 1 clove garlic
- 2 tablespoons olive oil
- ½ tablespoon tomato purée
- 2 teaspoons lemon juice
- ¼ teaspoon oregano
- Pinch sage
- Salt and freshly ground black pepper

Peel the tomatoes (see page 175), remove the seeds and chop the flesh. Peel and finely chop the onion. Squeeze the garlic through a garlic press. Heat the olive oil in a saucepan, add the onion and garlic and cook over a medium high heat for about three minutes until the onion is soft and transparent. Add the tomatoes, tomato purée, lemon juice and herbs and season with salt and freshly ground black pepper. Bring to the boil, cover and simmer for 20 minutes.

Tomato Sauce Made from Tinned Tomatoes

- 1 onion
- 1 clove garlic
- 1 tin tomatoes (8 oz)
- 2 teaspoons vinegar
- ¼ teaspoon oregano
- Pinch sage
- Pinch basil
- Salt and freshly ground black pepper

Peel and finely chop the onion. Squeeze the garlic through a garlic press. Heat the olive oil in a saucepan, add the onion and garlic and cook over a medium high heat until the onion is soft and transparent – about 3 minutes. Add the tinned tomatoes, vinegar and herbs, season with salt and pepper, bring to the boil, cover and simmer gently for 10 minutes.

Pickle Dressing

A sharp dressing to make an interesting change for summer salads.

- 1 egg yolk
- 1 tablespoon French Dijon mustard
- ¼ pint olive oil
- 1 teaspoon vinegar
- 2 tablespoons sour cream
- 1 tablespoon Branston pickle
- Salt and pepper

Combine egg yolk and mustard and beat well with a wooden spoon. Add oil, drop by drop, beating all the time until each drop has been absorbed by the yolk/mustard mixture. When the dressing is thick, blend in the vinegar. Add sour cream and pickle and season if necessary with salt and pepper.

Lemon & Egg Sauce

2 eggs
2 tablespoons lemon juice
½ pint chicken stock
Salt and pepper

Beat the eggs until thoroughly blended. Add lemon juice a few drops at a time. Blend in the stock and heat through over a *very low* heat, stirring continually until the sauce is the consistency of single cream. Season with salt and pepper.

Serve with chicken, lamb or fish.

Lemon & Mustard Sauce

2 cloves garlic
1 teaspoon dry mustard
2 tablespoons lemon juice
4 tablespoons olive oil
1 tablespoon finely-chopped parsley
Salt and pepper

Crush the garlic and mix with the mustard and lemon juice. Gradually add the oil, beating well. Mix in the parsley and season with salt and pepper.

Serve cold with grilled chicken, fish or meat.

Apple Sauce

2 large cooking apples
3 tablespoons water
Juice ½ lemon
2 tablespoons sugar
½ oz butter
Salt and pepper
Pinch powdered ginger

Peel, core and roughly chop the apples and put them into a saucepan with the water, lemon juice and sugar. Bring to the boil and simmer gently until the apples are quite soft – about 10 minutes. Purée the apples in an electric liquidizer, through a food mill or a fine sieve and return to a clean pan. Beat in the butter, season with salt and pepper and flavour with a pinch of ginger. Heat through before serving.

Serve with pork, bacon or gammon dishes, with sausages, roast duck or goose.

Variations

For an extra flavour add a pinch of sage and thyme to the sauce while the apples are cooking.

For an unusual savoury taste, add a little horseradish sauce to the apple sauce when it is being re-heated.

Orange Sauce to Serve with Duck

2 oranges
1 tablespoon olive oil
1 teaspoon cornflour
Juice 1 lemon
2 teaspoons brown sugar

Peel the oranges, divide into segments and remove any white membrane. Cut the segments into ½ inch pieces. Heat the olive oil in a saucepan, add cornflour and cook, stirring over a medium heat until the mixture is smooth. Blend in the lemon juice and brown sugar and continue to stir until the sugar has melted. Add the orange segments and heat through.

Aspic Jelly

Home-made aspic jelly involves a lengthy cooking and straining process. In these days of busy housewives, many of whom are working, I would recommend using packet aspic crystals or, better still, the tinned consommé produced by Crosse & Blackwell; if it is well chilled, the soup will jellify well and makes a good alternative to the real thing.

Add a little lemon juice and dry sherry to aspic crystals or tinned consommé to give an extra flavour. A spoonful of tomato purée added to the mixture gives a pleasant reddish tinge.

Puddings which you can enjoy without regretting later

Puddings for anyone with a weight problem (or a potential weight problem) are a problem. Usually, they fall into one of four categories; rich pastry sweets, puddings made with lashings of cream, fruit sweets in heavy syrups or those marvellous nursery favourites thick with bread, cake or custard. All these are disastrous to the figure and should be avoided at all costs. If necessary, avoid the temptation altogether and stick to cheese with a plain water biscuit or to fresh fruit.

If you cannot bear to live your life without a pudding or dessert, then choose one which has a fruit base, is made without an excessive quantity of sugar, starch or cream and steer clear of all pastry ingredients.

It isn't too depressing; there are a number of puddings which are not, weightwise, catastrophic and I hope the following recipes may give some ideas of the sort of recipes to choose.

September Melons

Blackberries are at their height in September (in Cornwall they warn not to pick them after 1 October because on that day the Devil spits on the fruit). Happily, this is also a time when Ogen and Charantais melons should be at their lowest in price. Combine the two and you have a really delicious sweet which, if the blackberries are plump and ripe, should need very little extra sugar.

1 lb blackberries
2 tablespoons caster sugar
2 teaspoons lemon juice
2 medium large (or 4 small) Ogen or Charantais melons
⅛ pint port (optional)

Pick over the blackberries and wash them only if absolutely necessary. Put the berries into a bowl, sprinkle with sugar and lemon juice and mix lightly without bruising the fruit. Chill in the refrigerator for an hour. Halve the large melons (or cut a slice from the top of the small melons), scoop out the pips and fill the cavities with the blackberries. Pour over the port, if used.

Note: The flavour of all fruit (except that picked and eaten on the spot) is improved by it being served chilled. The smell of melons, however, is so strong that if they are to be chilled in a refrigerator they must be sealed in a polythene bag to prevent other foods being tainted. As an alternative to this, the melons can be served on a bed of crushed ice.

Passion Fruit Fool

Not long ago it was difficult to find passion fruit in any but the most expensive fruiterers in London. Now I can buy them in my small country shop and, although their price varies a lot, these sharp, delicious, tropical fruit are not unreasonable at the height of the season. For a quickly-made pudding this Passion Fruit Fool has a lot going for it. Not the least fattening of sweets but so good it is worth cutting down on something else in order to justify an intake of sugar and cream.

12 passion fruit
4 oz caster sugar
½ pint double cream
2 oz chopped, blanched, almonds

Cut the tops off the passion fruit and scoop out the insides. Add sugar and mix well. Beat cream until stiff and fold in the fruit. Pile into four wine glasses or goblets and chill in a refrigerator. Roast almonds in a hot oven (425°F, Reg 7) for about 2 minutes until golden brown. Cool and sprinkle over the fool just before serving.

Tangerine Flummery

This is a marvellously light and airy pudding and, although it is made with a fair proportion of sugar, the final mixture is so bulky that you end up by eating only a minute proportion. The secret of its success lies in continuing to beat the egg yolks while adding the hot sugar syrup in a slender stream – this can only be done by using an electric whisk or having a helper.

¼ pint water
8 oz sugar
Juice and grated rind 4 tangerines
Juice 1 lemon
4 eggs, separated
1 tablespoon blanched, roasted and crushed almonds

Combine the sugar and water in a saucepan, bring to the boil and cook over a high heat for fifteen minutes. Beat the egg yolks until pale and fluffy. Gradually beat in the hot sugar syrup, whisking continuously, and continue to beat until the mixture is cold. Blend in the tangerine juice and add the rinds. Whisk the egg whites until stiff and fold them into the yolk mixture. Pour into a souffle dish or glass bowl and chill at least an hour before serving.

Sprinkle roasted crushed almonds over the top.

Serves 6–8

Fresh Pear Dessert

Sometimes recipes seem almost too simple to mention in a cookery book. This is just such a dish and I might have ignored it altogether had I not recently noticed a gentleman in one of the most expensive restaurants in London enjoying pears prepared in this way as though it were one of the greatest luxuries in the world. For those with an eye on their waistlines who nevertheless like to round off a meal with a dessert this is the perfect answer.

Juice 2 lemons
Pinch cinnamon
Pinch ginger
4 ripe eating pears

Combine the lemon juice, cinnamon and ginger and mix very well. Heat in a saucepan over a low flame for 2 minutes to bring out the flavour of the spices and leave to cool. Peel the pears, cut them in half, remove the cores and arrange them flat side down on a serving dish. Pour over the spiced lemon juice and chill for ten minutes before serving.

Winter Fruit Salad I

Fresh fruit salads are always popular with both adults and children. Often they tend to be thought of as a summer pudding but a good winter variety can be made from seasonable fruit, nuts and dried fruit. This particular pudding, by the way, has a good leavening of vitamin C to keep away winter colds.

2 oranges
1 tangerine
2 large Cox's apples
1 pear
2 oz dates
2 oz dried apricots (soaked, to swell up, if preferred)
2 oz cashew or chopped brazil nuts
Juice 2 oranges
Juice ½ lemon
4 tablespoons coarse brown sugar

Peel the oranges, remove any white pith and membrane and

thinly slice the flesh, removing any pips. Peel and thinly slice the tangerine. Peel, core and dice the apples and pear. Remove the stones from the dates and finely chop the flesh. Finely chop the apricots. Combine all the fruit and nuts in a serving bowl, pour over the fruit juice and sprinkle over the sugar. Chill before serving.

Serves 4–5

Note: This fruit mixture also makes a delicious, non-fattening start to the day if served instead of cereal.

Winter Fruit Salad II

In the winter one sometimes longs for those steaming nursery puddings of days gone by; a yellow sponge dripping with golden syrup, bread and butter pudding with thick cream or a good old-fashioned Queen of Puddings. This may not have the warmth of those old favourites but it is extremely satisfying and you won't regret having eaten it later.

3 tangerines or 6 small clementines
1 pear
2 eating apples
6 dates
$\frac{1}{4}$ pint fresh orange juice
1 tablespoon Bacardi rum
2 oz cashew nuts

Peel and thinly slice the tangerines. Peel, core and slice the pear. Peel, core and thinly slice the apples. Remove the stones if necessary and chop the dates. Combine the fruit and nuts in a serving dish, pour over the orange juice and Bacardi and chill well before serving.

Uncooked Orange Cheesecake

4 oz ginger biscuits
2 oz unsalted butter
2 eggs
½ lb soft cream cheese
2 tablespoons lemon juice
1 tablespoon gelatine
⅛ pint water
4 tablespoons sour cream
2 oranges

Crush the ginger biscuits, mix them with the butter and press the mixture into the sides and bottom of a lightly-greased flan case. Bake the case in a moderately hot oven (400°F, Reg 6) for 8 minutes, leave to cool in the tin and turn out carefully.

Beat the egg yolks and blend them with the cream cheese until smooth. Add the lemon juice and mix well. Soften the gelatine in the water over a low heat and beat into the cheese mixture. Blend in the sour cream. Beat the egg whites until stiff and fold them lightly into the cream cheese mixture. Peel and very thinly slice the oranges. Arrange half the slices in the bottom of the biscuit case, cover with the cheesecake and leave in a cool place to set. When set cover the top with the remaining orange slices.

Serve well chilled.

Gooseberry Sherbet

½ pint water
4 oz sugar
1 lb ripe gooseberries
1 tablespoon lemon juice
1 egg white

Combine the water and sugar, bring to the boil and simmer for 5 minutes. Add the gooseberries and cook for about 10 minutes until soft. Cool and purée in an electric liquidizer, through a food mill or a fine sieve and mix in the lemon juice. Pour into ice-making trays and freeze until the mixture begins to crystallize around the edges. Turn into a bowl and beat to a smooth mush with a rotary whisk. Beat the egg white stiff and fold it into the gooseberry purée. Return to the ice-making trays and freeze until firm – about 4 hours.

Serve in chilled glass goblets.

Caribbean Fruit Mousse

A rather sharp mousse and not for anyone who has a sweet tooth. This is a particularly good pudding to follow a rather heavy or rich main course.

5 large eggs
4 oz caster sugar
1 tablespoon (½ oz) gelatine
Finely-grated rind and juice 1 lemon
Juice 1 large grapefruit
1 small tin pineapple pieces

Separate the eggs and beat the yolks with the sugar until pale yellow and fluffy. Dissolve the gelatine in the lemon juice over a low heat until melted. Add the gelatine mixture, grapefruit juice and finely-grated lemon rind to the egg yolks and mix well. Leave until cold and beginning to thicken slightly. Drain the syrup from the pineapple pieces and mix them into the mousse. Whisk the egg whites until stiff, lightly fold them into the mousse and pour it into a serving dish. Chill in a refrigerator for at least two hours until set firm.

White Wine Jelly with Black Grapes

A pretty summer pudding with a pleasantly sharp tang to it.

1 tablespoon (½ oz) gelatine
Juice ½ lemon
1 tablespoon sugar
¾ pint dry white wine
½ lb black grapes

Combine the gelatine with the lemon juice, sugar and 3 tablespoons white wine and heat over a low flame until the gelatine is dissolved. Cool and combine with the rest of the wine. Leave until the jelly is beginning to thicken. Halve the grapes, remove the pips and put them in a glass bowl. Pour the wine jelly over the grapes and leave in a cold place to set.

Orange Jelly

Although simple to make, this sweet looks pretty and tastes wonderfully fresh.

3 oranges
¾ pint fresh orange juice
1 tablespoon (½ oz) gelatine
Juice ½ lemon

Peel the oranges, remove all the pith and white membrane and cut them into very thin slices. Remove the pips and arrange the slices in a glass bowl. Soften the gelatine in 3 tablespoons orange juice over a low heat, add it to the rest of the orange juice and mix well. Stir in the lemon juice and pour the jelly over the oranges. Leave in a refrigerator until set.

Melon and Mint Jelly

Ogen and Charantais melons, which are available for a good many months of the year, are sweet enough not to heed the addition of any sugar. In this recipe, they are combined with mint to make a fresh-tasting summer pudding.

1 large ripe Ogen or Charantais melon
3 tablespoons finely-chopped mint
1½ tablespoons (¾ oz) gelatine
¼ pint water
Juice 1 lemon

Halve the melon, scoop out the seeds, retaining as much juice as possible. Scoop out the flesh with a ball scoop and reserve all the juice. Soak the mint leaves in the lemon juice for 30 minutes. Place the melon balls in a glass serving dish. Combine the gelatine and water and heat over a low flame until the gelatine has melted. Combine the gelatine mixture, lemon juice and mint and pour over the melon balls. Chill in a refrigerator until set firm.

Melon Masquerade

1 ripe honeydew melon
½ lb strawberries
1 tablespoon (½ oz) gelatine
¾ pint orange juice

Cut the melon in half, remove the seeds and scoop out the flesh with a ball scoop. Divide the strawberries and melon balls between the two half melon shells. Dissolve the gelatine in a little of the orange juice over a low heat. Add the gelatine to the remaining orange juice and leave to cool. Pour the jelly over the fruit and place the melon shells in the refrigerator until set firm.

Cut into thick slices to serve.

Serves 6

Apple Jill

A delicious way of cooking apples that brings out their flavour and makes a really perfect finish to a meal.

6 Cox's or other firm eating apples
1 pear
½ pint orange juice
Pinch cinnamon

Peel, core and slice the apples. Peel, core and slice the pear. Arrange the fruit in a lightly-buttered baking dish. Mix the cinnamon with the orange juice and pour it over the fruit. Bake the apples in a very moderate oven (350°F, Reg 4) for 30 minutes until the fruit is tender but not mushy.

Serve hot or cold.

Maidenwell Junket

Why do some people turn up their noses at junket? Properly made and served icy cold it makes one of the lightest and most pleasurable of summer puddings especially if served with freshly-picked fruit like strawberries, raspberries or blackberries sprinkled with a little lemon juice. Avoid the temptation to heap on to the surface of the junket the traditional Devonshire cream.

In this recipe the roasted almonds on top give it a pleasant crunchy taste.

2 pints milk
1 tablespoon rennet
1 tablespoon icing sugar
$\frac{1}{8}$ pint brandy
2 oz slivered, blanched almonds

Heat the milk to blood temperature. Pour it into a glass bowl and mix in the rennet, sugar and brandy. Leave to set in a warm place. Roast the almonds in a hot oven (425°F, Reg 7) for 2 minutes until golden brown. Cool and sprinkle over the set junket. Chill the junket for 20 minutes before serving.

Serves 6

Grapefruit and Orange Jelly

2 grapefruit
1 tablespoon (½ oz) gelatine
1 tablespoon sugar
½ pint orange juice
¼ lb grapes

Peel the grapefruit and remove the skin and membrane from the segments. Arrange the segments in a shallow glass serving dish. Combine the gelatine with the sugar and about 4 tablespoons orange juice and heat over a low flame until the gelatine has melted. Combine the gelatine mixture with the remaining orange juice and leave until cool and just beginning to set. Pour the jelly over the grapefruit and leave in a refrigerator to set firm. Halve the grapes and remove the pips. Garnish the set jelly with grapes.

Melon Tout Suite

One of the most delicious ways of serving melon. One of those luscious but so often expensive Charantais or Ogen melons can be stretched to serve four or six people if used in this recipe and the surrounding jelly if anything enhances the flavour of the fruit.

Juice and grated rind 1 lemon
2 tablespoons sugar (or sugar substitute)
2 tablespoons hot water
1 packet (½ oz) gelatine
½ pint dry white wine
1 ripe Charantais or Ogen melon
A few black grapes for decoration

Combine lemon juice, lemon rind, sugar, water and gelatine in a saucepan and heat gently until gelatine and sugar are both melted. Add white wine and chill until the jelly begins to thicken. Halve melon and remove seeds. Remove the rind and cut the flesh into small cubes. Add the melon to the jelly and pour into a serving dish. Chill until set firm and decorate with peeled halved grapes with the pips removed.

Serves 4–6

Index